Spark: The Complete Public Relations Guide for Small Business

Hundreds of easy and practical PR ideas you can use today to win media visibility, power up your communications and beat the competition! Great for non-profits and other organizations too.

By Robert Deigh

ISBN-13: 978-1973721956

ISBN-10: 1973721953

Contents

4

Introduction

Information is a commodity. It's everywhere. Thus, our ability to sort through all of the messages we receive daily -- to piece together *real, useful knowledge* -- and educate ourselves for work, family or other interests, has become increasingly difficult.

How much information do we receive on an average day? Estimates vary widely– from 1,500 messages to a staggering 20,000. They include media stories, social media posts, ads, movies, TV shows, podcasts, books, commercials, signs, texts, emails, packaging, bumper stickers, billboards, store displays, street signs, logos, direct mail and, of course, the book you are holding in your hand.

Here's an amazing fact. Even before the advent of the web, the amount of information available to us was massive. According to Paul B. Brown and Alison Davis, in their book, *Your Attention, Please*, "a typical issue of *The New York Times* contains more information than the average person in the 17th Century was likely to encounter during his lifetime."

Provide Valuable and Welcomed Information

If you run a business or other organization, you don't want to contribute to the noise. You want to get positive attention by providing *valuable and welcomed information* – educating and interesting your most important audiences whether through the news media or directly.

That brings us to public relations -- the art of targeting useful information to specific audiences. Smart PR helps shine a light on the value of any organizations' products and services and helps them grow. That's the reason virtually all successful companies and non-profits use public relations as part of their outreach. It works.

Spark: The Complete Public Relations Guide for Small Business is written and organized to help you get attention by using smart, easy and proven PR tactics to win visibility without spending a lot of time or money. Each chapter presents proven methods I have used, and have seen many others use successfully, during more than 25 years as a journalist and public relations professional for companies like America Online, PBS, U.S. News & World Report, the U.S. Army, the federal government, PR firms and in my own PR practice.

How to use this book

1) The 23 chapters in this book each are organized like recipes in a cookbook. Only use what you need right now, whether it is a press release template, strategies on how to get your story told in the press, creating strong messages, learning how to do interviews, getting visibility at a trade show or simply writing compelling language into your website or social media. Maybe you have a big opportunity coming up that can raise your visibility if you can get people to pay attention. Or maybe you have a story idea you'd like to pitch to your newspaper or post on your own website. Turn to Chapters 10 and 11. You'll find those sections packed with ideas that will get you the attention you want. Or you might just need to write killer press releases that get read and published. That's Chapter 6. If you are participating in an industry event soon, flip to Chapter 21 on winning big at trade shows, and Chapter 20 on the fine art of networking.

2) Or, read the book from start to finish (but don't peek at the last page until you get there), adding layers of tactics on top of each other – chapter by chapter -- to learn to conduct a complete and tailor-made public relations plan for you and your organization. Many chapters have worksheet pages at the end so you can make notes that address your specific PR needs.

No Experience Needed

This book is designed primarily for people with little to no experience in public relations. But there are also plenty of great tips and tricks in these pages for PR and marketing professionals who want to expand their PR knowledge and toolboxes. It provides a logical, step-by-step approach to help you prioritize goals; understand how PR, the news media, and the tools of communication work; and help you determine what reporters and other audiences really want to know about you.

SPARK will teach you how to be a great storyteller. It's much easier than you think and can make the whole PR process highly effective and, frankly, a lot more fun. In short order, this book will help you win higher visibility in the marketplace.

Great companies – large and small – know how to use PR effectively to make a big impression. This book will help you do the same.

Welcome!

Public Relations:
Why This Stuff Really Works!

"The concept is interesting and well-formed, but in order to earn [a grade] better than a 'C,' the idea must be feasible." **-- a Yale University professor responding to undergrad Fred Smith's paper proposing a dependable overnight-delivery service (Smith went on to found FedEx).**

Chapter Summary: Why PR Works So Well and How You Can Use it to Succeed

Just a few years ago, if reporters were not interested in what you had to say, you were just out of luck. Today you can reach your audiences directly in powerful ways without going through traditional news media if you choose. Your ideas and opinions can go straight to intended recipients via social media (that we'll discuss in Chapter 8) such as blogs, email newsletters and podcasts. You can now be a publisher at little or no cost except the time you are willing to spend creating content. This book will show you how to do that.

None of this means we don't need to court the news media, of course. The media are still very important vehicles for communication. Therefore, most of this book is designed to giving you the skills and the confidence you will need to get strong media exposure.

Also, traditional papers and magazines have embraced social media, of course (virtually all have their own websites, apps and blogs), adding to our opportunities for winning coverage. The media are now our partners in publishing. It's the first time this has happened since Thomas Jefferson coined the phrase "public relations" in a speech back in 1807.

Why does PR work?

- Media stories carry credibility. A positive mention in a respected publication implies an objective endorsement by the publication whereas an advertisement, for example, does not.

- Social media gives you a voice that just a few years ago belonged only to prominent journalists – people who buy ink by the barrel.

- Media exposure is powerfully self-perpetuating. People see your name in publications or in web searches and it bestows upon you a mantle of expertise. Then, in turn, they want to call you for your opinion, which leads to more exposure. Greater exposure leads to getting quoted more often in the press.

- PR is much less expensive than advertising.

- You are seen as an opinion leader in your industry.

- It opens doors for you to sell products and services, and influence public opinion.

- It protects and enhances your reputation.

- It educates your audiences.

One of the funniest things I've ever heard in business came from a 20-something CEO of a startup company seeking venture capital. The company had yet to create a marketable product, find a customer, or make a penny. At a pitch meeting with about a half-dozen people, the young exec said with gravity about his company, "We have a combined quarter decade of experience." Let that sink in for a minute.

Telling Your Story is Powerful

Today, real companies — whether led by savvy millennials or veteran entrepreneurs — need real vision, a marketable product or service, a good team, and *the ability to tell a story* in a way that provides high VISIBILITY. Positive and consistent visibility makes prospects want to learn more about you and your organization.

Many of my clients over the years have been small or medium-sized companies with good products or services that, at least initially, few people had heard of—your classic tree falling in the forest. If their potential customers just knew about them, they'd certainly be interested. The trick is getting the word out. Building positive "buzz" in the marketplace is both affordable and doable for even the most budget-conscious business.

The same goes for nonprofit organizations that are trying to increase membership and promote issues, companies launching a new product or service, and military and government organizations fulfilling their missions. Maybe you've decided that now is the time to break out of the pack and become the "go-to" organization in your industry. This book will help you do that.

What is Public Relations?

PR is not "free media." Just because you don't pay money to get a story in your local city paper does not mean it's free. Getting visibility via media placement takes time, some resources at least, and something newsworthy to offer the reader. But, dollar for dollar, hour for hour, PR is very cost-effective and anyone can make it work

Public relations is a powerful force that influences the way in which the public regards individuals, organizations, and ideas. As its name implies, the focus of PR is to build positive and productive relationships between various parties. The Public Relations Society of America says that PR "helps our complex, pluralistic society to reach decisions and function more effectively by contributing to mutual understanding among groups and institutions. It serves to bring private and public policies into harmony."

Also it's important to know what public relations is not. PR is not sales. It is not business development. It is not marketing. But it strongly supports all of those functions in any organization. More and more companies are turning away from traditional advertising (paid media) and putting more of their budget into "earned" media— that is, public relations. You create a brand with public relations. You grow and defend it with advertising, marketing, and continued public relations.

PR vs. Paid Advertising

For the same cost as a quarter or half-page ad in a top-10 daily newspaper, for example, a small company on a budget can put a fair amount of resources into public relations activities, whether they do the work themselves or hire it out. Consider that a one-time ad insert, even a full page, is generally wasted. Repetition is critical to effective advertising. Companies spend millions of dollars over a relatively long period to run ads repeatedly in the media.

Let's consider, for example, a small ad in a magazine published by any major city's daily paper – maybe a fifth of a page. To get real attention, you'd need to run it repeatedly. If you paid for 12 ads that size, each would cost you about $10,000 (a volume discount), for a total of $120,000.

Now, take that same fifth of a page and imagine it is part of a news story on your industry. And in that same fifth of a page, you—or even better, an unbiased industry expert—are quoted praising your company or products. Placement in the news story is many times more believable than the ad.

Which would likely make you run out and buy a new model of laptop: praise by the Wall Street Journal and Consumer Report or an ad for the product? Reporters are considered unbiased experts and we trust them for the most part to do the homework and research we don't have the time and expertise to do ourselves.

Expertise has become very specialized. Robert Parker, for example, is considered the dean of wine critics. A comment in his newsletter or in one of his dozen or so books can make or break the sale of a wine brand. An ad could rarely if ever ignite the same fire. Public relations opens the door to visibility.

Restaurants across the country are full of waiters bursting with talent—real talent—singers, dancers, actors, and musicians. But we'll see few of them on the screen or stage, of course, because they won't get The Big Break—that meeting with an industry big shot, that article or TV spot that will attract the attention of someone who can elevate them to success. The same goes for great companies and other organizations.

There are plenty of them out there with spectacular products and services that you and I would gladly pay for if only we knew about them. But without exposure to the right audiences, the companies will remain invisible and, eventually, go under.

Know Who You are Trying to Reach? Go Get 'Em

Whether you are part of a small to midsize organization, an entrepreneur, or anyone with public relations responsibilities, this book is for you. ***Spark: The Complete Public Relations Guide for Small Business*** includes every tool you need to get attention from the audiences that matter most to you, whether they are customers, sales prospects, the news media and other opinion leaders, investors, employees, or vendors. Understand your audiences. Before you proceed, prioritize them according to the ones that will have the greatest effect on your organization, your mission, your sales goals, and other objectives.

Your audiences can be some or all of these:

- Customers
- The news media
- Prospects
- Investors and lenders
- Employees
- Employee families and friends
- Partners
- Vendors
- Labor organizations
- Boards of directors
- Regulators
- Federal, state and local governments
- Trade associations
- Networking groups
- Competitors

Make an Emotional Connection to Your Customers

Using public relations is more often about making an emotional appeal to your audience rather than addressing only logic. The use of hybrid cars, better health care, more medical research, more accountability in government, and safe playgrounds are all issues that have benefited from an emotional appeal using public relations.

Does your product or service hit them right in the heart when it counts? During a natural disaster, for example, can you provide help? Are you a radio station with information, a facility with shelter and food, or a company that offers medical assistance or transportation? (Think of snow days in which people with SUVs race to hospitals, shuttling doctors and nurses to work.)

Whatever you are promoting, you need to explain to your audiences on an emotional level how it benefits them or others they care about.

Every good product, every good service is, at its heart, a means by which to help people live, work, or play better. As retailers know, what they sell are benefits, not features.

Travel agents sell adventure, discovery, education, and relaxation (not trips); movie theaters sell escape, romance, and excitement; software makers sell efficiency and convenience; jewelers sell glamour and love; home builders sell togetherness, shared lives, and community; luxury carmakers sell power and status; restaurants sell taste experiences and camaraderie; and fashion designers sell style, beauty, and sex.

If you sell office supplies, you are really selling efficiency. Violins? A lifetime of musical enjoyment. Hybrid cars? Good environmental practices, cost savings, and trendiness. Has anyone ever bought a top-of-the-line Harley Davidson motorcycle just for sheer transportation, or a $20,000 Breitling watch just to tell time?

People trust brands, and brand building comes about as the result of marketing and public relations, supported by advertising and word of mouth. A good brand provides buyers with predictable quality. And, in the war for attention, brands win. You can be the top brand, even if it is only within your industry or among your target audiences. This book provides the tools that you will use to make your case, personalize what you do, and help people understand clearly on an emotional and rational level the benefits you can provide.

People respond appeals that address one or more of needs:

- **Business/mission:** Can you help them meet their goals, make more money, save time, get a promotion or beat their competitors?

- **Self-improvement:** Can you provide the means by which your audience can be better informed, more fit, less stressed, more aware and more marketable?

- **Social life/lifestyle:** Can you make their lives more enjoyable, provide more leisure time, make them more attractive, help them find romance, make them healthier or help them further their hobbies or other avocations?

- **Reputation:** Can you further enhance or protect their professional or personal reputations?

- **Beliefs:** Can you provide a place, physical or virtual, where they can express opinions, beliefs, or other personal feelings? Does your organization support a cause in which they strongly believe? Can you help them connect with others like themselves, or give them a place where they can experience diversity and meet people who are unlike themselves?

- **Philanthropic:** Can you help them to help others and also feel good about themselves?

- **Fantasy/Escape:** Can you help them get away from the mundane and routine?

If you can address one or more of these needs on an emotional level, you have a much better chance of having people understand what you can provide and respond favorably to it. They will be more willing to take an action you would like them to take.

Worksheet: Audiences

Our Most Important Audiences Are:

1.

2.

3.

4.

5.

Worksheet: Connections

How Does Our Organization Make Emotional Connections with Our Audiences? How Do We Make Their Lives Better?

1.

2.

3.

Winning Visibility:
12 Rules You Must Know

"I know only two tunes. One is 'Yankee Doodle,' and the other isn't." -- **Ulysses S. Grant, responding to a reporter's question about the general's taste in popular music**

Chapter Summary: Don't Make the Same Mistakes Your Competitors Make

1. Know your customers: who they are, how they think, and what they need.
2. Create a set of five or six messages that tell all of your audiences, in plain English, the benefits you provide.
3. Personalize your organization. People relate to people, not organizations.
4. Network like it's part of your job, because it is. Be visible in the marketplace.

5. Determine which PR tools can help you reach your business goals.

Before you set out to increase the public profile of your organization take a minute to spot your biggest shortfalls, the kinds of things that can keep you from rising above your competition and getting noticed.

Here are 12 traits that companies with excellent visibility have in common. Check off the ones you have already accomplished and rate yourself on a scale of 1-10 with a 10 being "We've Got That Covered" and a 1 being "Wait. What?"

1. We know our top customers as individuals not just as professional acquaintances. We know their backgrounds, interests, whether they are married, whether they have children, their hobbies, the magazines they read, and where they vacation. (These kinds of things come up naturally in conversation. Remember them.)

How to we rate 1-10? _____

2. We know our customers' "pain points," their biggest problems. We understand how to help solve those problems and we can communicate problem-solving abilities to our customers.

How to we rate 1-10? _____

3. Everyone in our organization uses the same talking points to communicate with our audiences. Our informal and formal communication is conducted in plain English without industry jargon. We can all explain accurately what we do.

How to we rate 1-10? _____

4. We have an active press campaign and get at least some regular coverage in the news media.

How to we rate 1-10? _____

5. We have personalized our organization, our products, our services, or our issues. (Surprise customers by sending notes to thank them for their support. Place photos of your employees on your website so people can associate faces with names. Network with your audiences at community and industry events. Overdeliver in such a way that customers can link the extra value they are getting to individuals on your team.)

How to we rate 1-10? _____

6. We have organized a successful trade show strategy that communicates, in a positive way, about our organization. We put as much work into following up with contacts after the show as we do in planning our participation.

How to we rate 1-10? _____

7. We have anticipated various crises. We have a good, concise PR plan for dealing with them and have practiced how to cope with the most likely scenarios.

How to we rate 1-10? _____

8. Our website and marketing/press/sales materials are up to date and reflect well on our organization. We understand and use some of the new social media tools.

How to we rate 1-10? _____

9. We keep up with news in our industry. We read the publications that our clients and competitors read. (Also read a couple of other publications that your competitors are likely to overlook. Good ideas for business and visibility can come from unlikely places.)

How to we rate 1-10? _____

10. We are active networkers.
How to we rate 1-10? _____

11. We have made diversity part of our PR strategy and we are visible in minority publications and minority organizations. (The Latino community, in particular, is growing rapidly and is such a big economic force that you should address it as a specific audience. The same goes for African-Americans, Asians, seniors, and the disabled).

How to we rate 1-10? _____

12. We have set realistic but worthwhile PR goals.

How to we rate 1-10? _____

Set Specific Goals and Let the Success Begin

Number 12 is in a class by itself. Before you embark on activities to increase your visibility through public relations, set some reachable goals for you and your team. Start the process by reviewing your overall business goals and decide which ones can be accomplished using PR tactics. Remember, public relations strongly supports sales and marketing, but it does not take the place of those two functions. For example, if one of your business objectives is "to increase sales by 15% over the next year,"

PR Goals That Can Support That Objective Include:

• Get our organization mentioned in 3-4 trend articles in our most important industry journals.

• Get one or two product reviews in the major trade publications our customers read.

• Develop relationships with the 4-5 top reporters in our industry.

• Get one or two byline articles published in our local business journal or in widely read trade publications.

• Create a website that customers and the news media will consider authoritative enough to visit for information about our industry even when they are not looking for information specifically about our company.

• Create an active blog to which our employees and customers can contribute and have it linked to a relatively wide network of other blogs and websites.

• Actively network with two or three organizations that will give us useful contacts and enable us to give back to our industry.

• Get our executives booked for two speaking engagements this year.

• Send an online newsletter to all of our contacts and get at least 30% readership (that's considered a strong open rate).

Reporters in the Wild:
A Field Guide

"Newspapers should have no friends." **-- Joseph Pulitzer**

Chapter Summary: A press interview is a business transaction.

1. A media interview is a business transaction, much like any other. Each party has something the other wants and needs.
2. Reporters today tend to be young, well educated and, for the most part, urbane. Understand what motivates them.
3. Before you contact reporters, read their articles and understand what they cover. Make sure you are giving them news not just information. Avoid contacting them near their deadlines.
4. The 24-hour news cycle provides the opportunity for just about anyone to be a journalist.
5. Go hear reporters when they speak on panels or at other events. It's a great way to meet them.

Imagine a room nearly the size of a city block, fluorescent tubes casting a yellow pall on every face and surface. Wood and metal desks are lined up back to back in long rows. On each desk is a manual typewriter and a telephone – a real, five-pound, push-button, black Ma Bell.

Everyone answers the phone on the first or second ring because, with no caller ID, it could be anyone -- your editor, someone with a juicy story to tell, a lover, or an invitation to an event with free food and beer.

A scratchy police scanner sits on the desk of the city editor with first responders talking through day and night. A haze of nicotine hangs just under the yellowed ceiling. But we're young and immortal and, besides, no one cares yet about the dangers of tobacco. In the corner of the room are two heavy and immovable olive-drab printers that belong to United Press International and The Associated Press, crackling out pages of news in real time. If you read the printouts as they emerge, you are one of the first people in the world to know practically everything.

This was the heart of the American newsroom, arguably unchanged in sight, sound and smell for 100 years -- from the late 1870s to the late 1970s. It was the most exciting place on earth to work, an experience that could spoil you for anything that was to come. To be young, working all night because a big front-page story was breaking, made you feel like a real journalist even if you were just a junior copy assistant.

On the way out in the morning you stop by the pressroom where men in inky overalls and newspaper hats feed car-sized rolls of Canadian paper into machines the size of houses. To walk home with that first edition of the newspaper under your arm was to feel like a true insider, impossibly important.

Back to the Future

There are still a few reporters old enough to remember those heady days. But today, real journalism belongs not only to reporters at established news organizations, but arguably, anyone with internet access and something to say. What's the difference between a reporter for The New York Times and a blogger with 20 years of experience – both of whom cover the same topic? In terms of knowledge, often nothing. In both cases, credibility has to be earned the hard way.

Who Loves Ya Baby?

Given all of the *armchair* journalists out there, do you get the feeling that the American public holds the *traditional* press in higher esteem than it did just a few years ago?

Me neither.

In a recent Gallup poll of trust among 21 professions, journalists ranked only in the middle of the pack. In order of preference, journalists rated above real estate agents, bankers, builders, lawyers, real estate agents, union leaders, business execs, stockbrokers, ad salespeople, car sales people, telemarketers (who, ironically, use the came cold calling methods as the pollsters who did this survey), members of Congress and lobbyists. At the top of the trust list, in order, are nurses, pharmacists, doctors, high school teachers, police officers, clergy, funeral directors and accountants. Make of that what you will.

Reporters in the wild have a lot of freedom. The sooner you accept that fact, the sooner you will be able to work in harmony with them. The reason is simple: journalists—or at least the work they do—are protected by nothing less than the First Amendment: "Congress shall make no law abridging the freedom of the press."

Even those who feel that they have been wronged by the press—or feel that it is too liberal or too conservative—agree that a free press is one of the great strengths of American democracy. And, in terms of influencing the way we think, journalists are at the top of the food chain right alongside elected officials and other opinion leaders.

I like reporters. Having been one, I appreciate the difficulty, frustrations, and importance of the job. Also, having worked with thousands of them from the other side of the fence, as a PR professional, I have learned to respect their intellectual curiosity, the power they have over public opinion, and, in turn, the influence they have on our culture.

They also drive me crazy. I often wish some could be better informed, more careful about checking facts, and more responsive.

Dealing with the press can be like having Sunday dinner with an eccentric uncle. For better or worse, pleasant or cranky, he's family and you have to tolerate him. I could not do my job without the news media.

Harvard Grads and Texans

Reporting for print or broadcast is a difficult job and not nearly as glamorous as it may appear. Most reporters across the country – are underpaid, slogging it out under intense deadline pressure for equally harried editors and producers—some of whom would make the biggest SOB on your staff blush. They get lied to by some of the best in the business and develop a shell that some people find difficult to penetrate. They are proud of what they do.

Like Harvard grads and Texans, if a person is a reporter, you'll know it within the first three minutes of a conversation. If he's a Harvard grad who reports for a Texas publication, you'll know sooner.

People like Jake Tapper, Anderson Cooper, Christina Amanpour and Chuck Todd are exceptions to the rule, of course. They are celebrities -- every bit as famous as many of the people they cover. Unless you are a VIP, a major newsmaker, or a celebrity in rehab, the chances of encountering them are fairly slim.

Traditional journalism is no longer a craft. It is a profession. Long gone are the days when young men or women (they were almost always men) started in the mailroom of a newspaper, chain-smoked their way onto the copy desk, moved into the newsroom, and later became bylined reporters. Getting a position at any publication or broadcast organization is hard, given their tough financial situation and the intense competition for few jobs. Ad pages are down in most publications and competition from the internet, of course, is a major factor.

Doing Well and Doing Good

Reporters today tend to be young, well educated, and, for the most part, urbane. They are either "beat" reporters who cover the same overall topic every day, "general assignment" reporters who cover virtually any topic of interest to readers, or columnists who tend to be more experienced and have earned that position after years of slogging it out as a reporter. But whether they are rookies or veterans, anonymous or famous, most reporters want the same things:

• The ability to affect change—doing good by doing well
• Their byline in print or their face on the air often
• Important assignments and scoops
• The approval of their editors and the admiration of colleagues and competitors
• Awards and other recognition for their work
• Invitations to important events where they can meet opinion leaders and celebrities
• The world's best cocktail-party stories

After more than 25 years in the communications business – as a reporter and in PR I have participated in hundreds of press interviews, from print and online to radio and TV. I have worked with reporters who were sharp, well-informed, as well as others who were ill-prepared, arrogant, or both. I have worked with executives who understand the value of the press and who are excellent communicators, others who consider a press interview a near-death experience.

This book will help you build productive and positive relationships with reporters and editors, the first step in building visibility through the media.

Stop the #%*@$ Presses!

First and foremost, news is a business and, like any other businesses, the successful ones watch their bottom lines closely. That is why deadlines in traditional media like newspapers and magazines are so important and unforgiving. Behind every reporter stands an editor who must go through the story and, in theory anyway, improve it. The graphics people must marry it up with charts and graphs, etc. Then the copy desk gives it a once-over to check facts, grammar, and spelling and write a headline.

If it's a paper product rather than internet-based, it then goes into page layout, into the presses, through the folding machines, and into the trucks that will have it at your door by 6 a.m. The fact that this happens every day is a minor miracle. You need to be familiar with this if you are going to deal with the press on a regular basis.

I learned the importance of this process early at my first job at a small 10,000-circulation weekly newspaper. An old Southern gentleman had written a long, heartfelt poem that we had planned to publish as the winning entry in a writing contest. It was my job to proofread the poem and make sure we got it into the paper just as the author had written it.

As the presses started rolling for that week's issue, I realized in horror that the typesetting machine had somehow lopped off the last third of the old man's poem. The moment I realized this, I ran in to the pressroom screaming— Hollywood style—over the roar of the huge machines, "STOP THE PRESSES! STOP THE PRESSES!" But before the press operators could even react to my idiotic tirade, the editor of the paper, hot on my heels, ran in roaring, "NO #*@&! WAY!!! Keep it rolling! Do not stop the presses!"

The cost of resetting everything would have been in the thousands of dollars—a lot for a tiny paper. It was left to me to call the old man and tell him that "we" had chopped off the back third of his poem. He was not impressed by my explanation about typesetting machines, deadlines, and trucks, etc., and was madder than hell at me for "hacking up" his work.

A Press Interview is a Business Transaction

A press interview is a business transaction, much like any other. Each party has something the other wants and needs. You can't get something without giving something in exchange. You want visibility. The reporter wants a story. That's the deal. And he or she does not want the room-temperature pabulum from your annual report. Think superlatives. Can you give a reporter something that makes your company or product first, best, biggest, smallest, most unique, quirky, funny, or controversial—(without doing harm to your company of course)? If so, you have a good story. You have something of value to trade with the reporter.

Fruitful relationships with the press must be based on mutual respect. Reporters need to know that you are telling them the truth even if you can't provide all of the information they want. You, in turn, need to be confident that the reporter's story—whether flattering, critical, or neutral—will be fair.

What Do Reporters Want?

This small section of the book will save you about $1,000, provide you with 20 hours of extra sleep this year, give you time for breakfast at home, and keep a lot of miles off of your poor beleaguered car. Honest.

I belong to a couple of PR industry groups. The local chapters each have one or two events a year on getting stories placed. The panels include reporters and editors; I've even moderated a few. After you have been to a couple you realize that virtually all reporters want the same thing if you are going to pitch them a story idea.

It can be summed up this way:

• Read my publication and familiarize yourself with what I write before calling me with a story idea.

• Make sure your idea has news value.

• E-mails are better than phone calls. I can look at the pitch and decide if I am interested. (If I am not, I might answer; I might not.)

• Don't send attachments with emails. Paste your information into the body of the email.

• Don't call to see if I got your news release. I got it. (More about this later.)

• Don't call me on deadline.

• Don't pitch the same story to my competitor. (Good name for a country song, I think.)

• Don't pitch the same story to another reporter on my paper until you give me a reasonable time to respond to your idea.

One of the best reasons to attend these events is to meet reporters face-to-face. My MO is to see who is on a panel, decide which of my clients has a story that would truly interest one or more of the reporters, bring a press release or fact sheet for the reporter and try to set up a meeting for a later date. This in-person approach can be very effective. By the time you follow up with them after the event, you are already preparing for what is, in essence, meeting number two.

The Death of Newspapers. Again?

Although it may seem like no one is reading newspapers in print any more, that's not yet the case. The Pew Research Center reported: "Although the public conversation about newspapers focuses on the shift to digital, most newspaper reading still happens in print. According to readership data from Nielsen Scarborough's Newspaper Penetration Report, 56% of those who consume a newspaper read it exclusively in print, while 11% also read it on desktop or laptop computers; 5% also read it on mobile; and another 11% read it in print, on desktop and on mobile. In total, more than eight-in-ten of those who read a newspaper do so in print, at least sometimes. Only 5% read newspapers exclusively on mobile devices."

But, I am confident that in a few years, newspapers and magazines will cease to exist, at least in paper form. They've been saying this for years, but the economics and environmental impact of printing on paper—in the face of competition from electronic media—are getting harder to ignore. The idea of buying paper by the multi-ton roll, printing it in giant plants, collating, folding, delivering, and having to recycle a newspaper is growing increasingly outdated.

Philip Meyer, a journalism professor at the University of North Carolina, and author of *The Vanishing Newspaper: Saving Journalism in the Information Age*, even goes so far as to predict the actual month and year of the death of the last newspaper: April 2040. Sounds overly optimistic to me. Whenever it happens, the decline will come gradually and be of surprise to no one.

Every morning I take a highly unscientific survey of the decline physical newspaper subscriptions. As I walk my dog through my neighborhood of about 140 houses, I notice that there is a steady drop in the number of newspapers in driveways. As I write this, only about two dozen people on my streets get a newspaper delivered to their house.

Sadly, in some cities, I'm afraid there are more people wearing the newspaper on a cold night than reading it.

There Will Always Be a Need for Skilled Editors

Technology may change but the need for sound news judgment will not. There will always be a place for reporters and editors—professionals with editorial judgment who can sift through mountains of information and select for us articles that will be of help and interest to us. Either they will actually choose the stories or they will make the daily decisions that affect the way news websites choose the stories for them, and for us.

What could be more daunting than having to sift through all of today's Associated Press wire stories and pick ones we want to read?

According to the Donald W. Reynolds National Center for Business Journalism at Arizona State University, "News judgment goes beyond merely defining the news as something "new" — important, timely, unique, having wide impact and (sorry "good news" apostles) conflict.

All those are important. But judgment goes deeper. It involves critical thinking, skepticism, analysis and context and the ability to set priorities about how reporting resources and news space (or online placement) will be best used. It depends on curiosity and a constant hunt for what lies beneath. Is the thing being pushed by a flack really news, and if so, how big? That "big scoop" may actually be a brief; a brief might conceal an important story. Tone, taste, fairness, accuracy and completeness all go into the decision-making process. So does play."

Create Messages That Make People
Sit Up and Take Notice

"Substitute 'damn' every time you're inclined to write 'very.' Your editor will
delete it and the writing will be just as it should be." -- **Mark Twain**

Chapter Summary: You Just Need Five or Six Messages

At a company where I worked, the CEO had an excellent way of getting employees to remember the company talking points (messages). He printed them up on plastic cards (about five to six of the main messages) and then distributed them to all staff members. He asked everyone to keep them in their wallets or purses. At the next all-staff meeting, he asked for a show of hands of staff members who had their message cards. Everyone who could produce a card was given a crisp $100 bill on the spot. At the next meeting, virtually everyone had the card and he handed out a stack of $20 bills. He never had to ask again.

Many organizations, large and small, public and private, don't communicate the benefits of products, services or causes in a way that can be understood clearly. Their communication is disorganized; no two parts of the organization are saying the same thing about the company to its principal audiences. The CEO is saying one thing (in speeches and media interviews), the sales team is saying something different (in client pitches, trade shows, and proposals), and the marketers are conveying something else. One of the main reasons for the disconnect is a lack of uniform and coherent messages and the ability to deliver them on target.

"What can you do for me?"

We're going to fix that. What customers and clients want to know more than anything else is, "What can you do for me?" The rest is just detail. It seems so obvious, but too many companies make you dig and dig into their websites, marketing materials, proposals, and presentations to get at that information. What they do instead is provide you with one-dimensional information about themselves.

This chapter is very important, and spending a few minutes here will build a foundation for all of your communication for months and years to come. A good set of clear messages is more powerful than 10 pounds of marketing materials. Get everyone on your team "on message" and get that language into all of your communication. Here's are elements of a four-part message document – a format that is easy to use:

- Part 1: The Company ID. List your organization's attributes. Use the important ones to create a 100-word paragraph about your organization that will resonate with customers. Use the text in all communication materials.
- Part 2: The elevator speech: a sentence or two that tells the listener, "Here is what I can do for you."
- Part 3: The must-say messages: the 5 or 6 main talking points that tell and sell your story.

- Part 4: Overall messages: 2-3 pages of detailed information about your organization, your product or service.

IMPORTANT: Before you start building your messages, make sure that everyone in your organization understands – with as much accuracy as possible – who you are trying to reach. Who are your audiences? Where do they shop? What do they buy? What are their important issues? To site one audience characteristic, for example, the primary age groups to consider are:

- **Traditionalists** (Born between 1925 and 1946)
- **Baby Boomers** (Born between 1946 and 1964)
- **Generation Xers** (Born between 1965 and 1980)
- **Generation Ys or Millennials** (born after 1980)

Here is what you want your messages to do: *Change your audience's thinking and behavior in a positive way that will cause them to take action that will directly benefit you and/or your organization and the people you serve.*

Whether you have four employees or 40,000, the ability of every member of your team to speak in a unified voice is a very powerful, competitive weapon. Creating effective messaging provides you and your team with a "codebook" to communication with any and all audiences: customers, potential customers, shareholders, vendors, investors, partners, employees and, of course, the news media. It provides a dramatic shortcut (a cut-and-paste sheet) for creating speeches, marketing materials, website text, news releases, and language for proposals, contracts, and other official communication.

The 4-Part Message Doc for Your Communications

A good format for a company message document is to divide it into four sections: 1) the Company ID, 2) the elevator pitch, 3) the "must-say" messages, and 4) the overall messages, the kind of information you want to keep close at hand (perhaps in a factsheet) but maybe not use in all communications.

The paper should be a simple text document that can be easily emailed to staff. It should be short enough to keep on any device, maybe two or three pages total. Don't worry about repetition; there will be overlap between the various parts of the message document. You need to make it as easy as possible for your team to cut and paste sections into any communication. Encourage team members to have these talking points available at all times even if you're not ready to hand out $100 bills.

Now let's create the four-part message document.

Message Document Part 1: Creating the Company ID

A boilerplate of about 100-200 words defines the company in a way that all audiences can understand. This can best be described as the "About Company XYZ" paragraph that is found at the bottom of news releases.

Creating a boilerplate forces members of the team to put in writing exactly what the company can do for clients: how they can help them save time, money, reputation, etc. They should create this paragraph from the point of view of client, in other words, "What can you do for me?"

Place this language on the front page of the website, at the top of proposals and presentations, at the bottom of news releases, and in any and all communication. It is important that the final product be compelling enough to get potential clients to call or visit your website. To create the Company ID, start by examining your own organization and providing answers to these kinds of questions:

- How do we differ from our competitors?
- What is the biggest customer problem we can solve?
- What have been our biggest successes?
- Why do customers choose us?
- How do we create value?
- How can we tie our products and services to those that people already know?

- How do our competitors view us?
- Why did we start this company?
- What is it like to work with our people?
- What do our customers think of us personally?
- What do our customers want that we have not yet provided?
- What advantages do we have over larger/smaller companies?
- Where do we want to be in a year?
- What news do we wish we could announce today that would give us higher visibility?
- Why have employees joined our company?

The best way to come up with a Company ID paragraph, at least one you can live with for a while, is to set up an informal brainstorming session. Gather the executive team in a comfortable room mid-morning when everyone is fresh. List the attributes of the company (answers to the questions above) on a whiteboard. There are no wrong answers at this point; they just need to be frank and specific to your company. Following are a few examples of attributes that other companies have come up with. (Try some of your own in the worksheet at the end of this chapter).

- Full-service
- Success for clients/customers
- Creative
- Strong established relationships in our industry
- Strong personal relationships with clients who refer us and come back repeatedly
- Ability to help you fulfill your mission
- Centralization of resources
- Top performer
- Save customers money
- Accountable for positive results
- Innovative thinkers, no cookie-cutter products
- Proactive
- Strong research capabilities
- Strong reputation—success stories
- Treat your budget as an investment

- Lower overhead

Most sessions produce about 50-100 attributes. Your mileage may differ. Now, choose the attributes that you feel are important to you and your audiences and knit them into a rough Company ID paragraph. For the company above, an early draft might sound something like:

"XYZ Co. is a full-service consulting firm that helps companies win and expand federal contracts. We have a 20-year track record of success in helping clients increase performance, save money, and lower overhead. Our team is made up of experts with decades of experience and extensive contacts in government, the private sector, and the military. XYZ Co. is a performance-oriented company with longstanding clients who depend on us to help carry out their missions. For more information, contact us at 555-555-5555 or visit xyz.com."

Creating the ID paragraph is often the most difficult part of the messaging exercise. Each person in the room will have a slightly different idea of what the company is and how to describe it. Come up with a draft ID that everyone in the room can accept at least temporarily. Then, have one person revise it to make it easily understood and compelling. One more round of comments should cement the language.

Message Document Part 2: Elevator Speech

Darth Vader's Pretty Good Elevator Speech

The Elevator Speech: Some people call this the "unique selling proposition." More executives have agonized unnecessarily over these few words than just about any other form of business communication. What do you say when you have 20 seconds with a potential buyer who can give you big business? How much detail should you provide? How long of a pitch do you give? If you have only two or three "floors" to make your pitch, and not a leisurely ride up to the 100th floor, have your elevator speech ready.

Here are some notable "elevator speeches" uttered on the silver screen -- movie lines that, if given in answer to the question -"So tell me, what do you do" -- would definitely get your attention:

• **"I'm an agent of chaos"** – Heath Ledger as Joker in *The Dark Night* (Batman)
• **"Luke, I am your father."** -- Darth Vader in *Star Wars*
• **"We rob banks."** -- Bonnie Parker in *Bonnie and Clyde*
• **"I see dead people."** -- Cole Sear in *The Sixth Sense*

To create a stop-'em-in-their tracks elevator speech, a compelling two or three sentences, you can borrow from your Company ID paragraph. Remember, you want to change your audience's thinking and behavior in a positive way that will cause them to take action that will directly benefit you and/or your company.

• Know your audience. Spend the first few moments learning about your "elevator" partners.

• Give them only the important attributes of your business: the ones that can benefit them the most. Remember, it's not really about YOU. *It's about what you can do for THEM.*
• Tell them how your company is different from those of your competitors and why they should hire you to help them succeed.

To Create A Good Elevator Speech:

• Use a shortened version of the Company ID paragraph as the starting point for your elevator speech. You've already spent the time and effort to define your company and the benefits it can provide. Use this information!

• Once you have an elevator speech that works, share it with your colleagues. There is nothing wrong with everyone using the same one if it works. In fact, having everyone using the same effective elevator speech is the point of creating one! A unified message is a powerful one.

In the case of XYZ Co., the elevator speech might sound something like:

"I work for a company that helps firms like yours win federal contracts. We've been around for 20 years and have helped our clients win millions of dollars in work. Let's meet if you have a few minutes so I can learn more about your company and how we can help you."

Here is another: "We help our clients win federal and state contracts. Our executives have extensive experience on senior-level government, military, and corporate projects, and can do what it takes to win and
keep major work."

Message Document Part 3: Must Say This!

Must-Say Messages. The Stuff to Memorize

Must-say messages are the 6-10 answers you will provide in any conversation about your company, regardless of the questions asked (we'll talk about "bridging" to these answers in Chapter 14). It may sound cynical to "bridge," but why would you even do an interview or write a byline article if not to leave your audience with at least a couple of convincing pieces of information about your organization? If, for example, you are giving a media interview, the main reason you are taking the time and effort of the interview is to get your messages into the story.

Write them down.

Let's try it. For XYZ Co., assume our must-say messages are:

• "We have a 20-year track record of success in helping companies win and expand federal contracts."
• "We win bids 85% of the time."
• "Our clients include Fortune 500 companies that have worked with us for 10 years or more."
• "Our clients really like us and would recommend us to anyone."
• "We tailor our products and services to each client."

OK, now for the interview and the art of hitting our must-say messages. We will go into more detail in Chapter 14 about doing interviews and speaking through the reporter, but for now, suffice it to say that you should not repeat a negative question (since it will end up as part of your answer) and be sure to hit your messages. Be concise, easily understood, quotable, and, above all, truthful. Answer the question, but do it on your terms, not the interviewer's.

Reporter: "Federal spending is on its way down. How can you possibly expect to grow in the next couple of years?"
You: "With two decades of success, and one of the most experienced teams in the industry, we've already weathered ups and downs. Our clients stay with us because we get results."

Reporter: "How come you lost the recent big Navy floating-widget contract?"
You: "We win the vast majority of the contracts that we go after. That's why we have government, military, and Fortune 500 clients who depend on us to help them succeed. We've done a lot of work for the Navy and have an excellent reputation there. There will be other good opportunities."

Reporter: "Yes, but that was an important contract."
You: "All contracts that we bid on are important to us and to the agencies we serve. That's why we have a team with more than 500 years of combined experience in senior-level government, military, and corporate experience. Our goal is to win and we do win the majority of the time."

Now, look at your answers. Is there anything there you'd rather not see in print? No, of course not. Each of your answers shows confidence and reflects well on your company while answering the questions and not being evasive. This kind of confidence is a magnet to potential customers. Imagine the same interview without clear messages—just giving the interview and hoping to come up with clever answers.

Here is one of the questions above. Now imagine seeing this answer in print.

Reporter: "How come you lost the recent big Navy floating-widget contract?"
You: "I guess our proposal was not good enough. Probably priced it too high as well." This answer does not reflect a sense of confidence, to say the least.

Message Doc Part 4: Everything Else

Overall Messages: the Big Picture of Your Organization

The overall messages (part #4 of your document) comprise a fact sheet, if you will, the full set of messages, the two or three pages of detailed language about your company, its team, its products, and its services that will provide a roadmap for your team to speak with a unified voice. It is the codebook that you and your staff can use to cut and paste language into all formal and informal communication.

Overall messages constitute a fairly detailed menu of approved language for everyone on your team. Remember, the whole document should not exceed three or four pages. Overall messages are a series of statements, each supported by a few proof points (important if you want your messages to be believable) about your organization. They might include your organization's successes, its attributes, its history, the qualifications of its team, its clients, its partners, its investors, its place in the industry, its wins in the market, and its sales figures.

The easiest place to start is to look back at the attributes you listed when working on the ID paragraph. Let's pick the first three and work from there. Here is how you might begin to construct the overall messages.

Full-Service

• XYZ Co. is a full-service company for any organization that seeks government work.

• We can provide all of the services that some organizations use two or three firms to provide.

• We have more than 500 years of combined experience in government, military, and the private sector.

Creative

• All of our services are in-house.

• We have a team of proposal writers that can help you win even the most complex RFPs.

• We have won awards for our creativity in creating attention-getting websites, marketing materials, trade show exhibits, events, and presentations. We'd be happy to provide references from other clients.
Strong, Established Relationships in Industry

• XYZ Co. is a performance-oriented and accountable company with longstanding clients who depend on us to help carry out their missions.

• We have strong relationships with all of the armed forces as well as most of the agencies of the executive branch.

• We have a 20-year track record of success in helping clients increase performance, save money, and lower overhead.

Put Your Message Document to Work

Using the message document is relatively simple. The CEO or another executive should present it to staff at an all-hands meeting as a tool to make staffers' jobs easier, not a manifesto that must be adhered to word-for-word. No more wondering, for example, what to say in a presentation.

It may sound trivial, but one of the people often overlooked in the messaging process is the company receptionist. Often, the receptionist is the first (or only) person a prospect might speak with in seeking information about your company. Make sure the receptionist can properly answer the question "What does your company do?" Instead of simply responding, "We're a software company," he or she might reply, "We are a software company that enables military, government, and law-enforcement agencies to increase efficiency while cutting information-technology budgets by an average of 20 percent." Put it in writing on a card at the front desk.

Do What They Don't Before They Do What You Do

Learn from your competitors and other companies that are similar in scope and size to yours. They have made plenty of mistakes by trial and error that you can avoid. Read any articles about them and see if the quotes reflect effective "messages." Do they help or hinder? Go on the Internet and review their news releases, executive bios, company statements, case studies, testimonials, and other communication. Do they portray a company that is innovative and inviting, or do their words just lie flat on the page?

If you are using effective messages that persuade, you have a big advantage over your competitor! Your products may be similar and your markets may be virtually the same, but the impression you leave on all of your audiences can be vastly different.

Worksheet: Attributes

As we discussed earlier in this chapter, "attributes" are the ingredients with which we create our messages. Write down a few of the qualities of your company – the stuff you like to brag about. Then pick the most important ones and use those to create your messages. I've included four examples to get you started.

1. Customers love to work with us
2. Highly experienced
3. Save customers an average of 15% in costs
4. On call 24/7
5. _____
6. _____
7. _____
8. _____
9. _____
10. _____
11. _____
12. _____
13. _____
14. _____
15. _____ 22
16. _____
17. _____
18. _____
19. _____
20. _____
21. _____
22. _____
23. _____
24. _____
25. _____

Easy Ways to Sharpen Your Organization's Writing and Make an Impact

"Long separated by cruel fate, the star-crossed lovers raced across the grassy field toward each other like two freight trains, one having left Cleveland at 6:36 p.m. traveling at 55 mph, the other from Topeka at 4:19 p.m. at a speed of 35 mph." **-- (From actual high school essays collected and shared by English teachers across the country).**

Chapter Summary: Better Writing = Better Communication = Higher Sales

1. Good business writing is just good writing.
2. Simplify. Simplify. Simplify!
3. Writer's block is a myth. Lower your standards and keep typing. You can edit it later.

4. Good business writing will help you rise above your competitors. Clarity will help your audiences understand you better and make them more inclined to give you a closer look.
5. Jargon, slang, and clichés are the enemies of good writing.
6. Edit your language for clarity and brevity.

Many people believe that the business they are in is so unique, so complex, that only people in the same business can truly understand it. That's a bit of self-flattery. It makes me wonder if NASA scientists ever say to each other, while waiting in a long cafeteria line to choose an entrée, "C'mon Chuck, pick something, will ya? This isn't rocket science." And then everyone chuckles for the hundredth time.

These are things I think about in the wee hours as I write this. Anyway, there is no topic that, to my knowledge, can't be explained satisfactorily to the rest of us in layman's terms: a self-driving car, plans to colonize Mars, a microchip, the War of 1812, the rise and fall of disco, DNA analysis, SuperPACs, NASCAR racing, and the appeal of playing cricket. OK, maybe not cricket. Or bagpipes.

People fall into flat language, clichés, and jargon for the same reason they wear bedroom slippers given to them during the Bush administration: They are comfortable and it takes effort and expense to acquire new ones. It takes a bit more effort to write clearly, but not too much more.

Whether you are writing a Declaration of Independence or a follow-up memo to a meeting, there are two reasons to pay attention to the clarity of your writing. First, if it's clear, people will actually read it – not a small consideration. Second, they will understand it and will be more likely to act on it.

The Way Words Taste

I love words. I love the way they travel through a good novel, a great quote, an insightful essay or movie dialogue. Well-written words are like themes and melodies in great music. Make flat or sharp only one or two notes in a chord or melody, and it can change the whole mood of the piece. Descriptive words have sensuality about them: the way they "taste" and feel in your mouth when you say them and the images they conjure up on a page.

For example, if I take a bite out of a big, ripe, yellow summer peach, the kind that drips juice all over the front of my chin and shirt, I would describe it as "luscious." Maybe "tasty" works, but that could also describe mashed potatoes. I could describe rollercoaster rides I took with my kids as "being strapped to a crazed rocket." Maybe "exciting" would do too, but that could also describe watching a baseball game (unless of course, it was watching the Boston Red Sox win the 2004 World Series, which was like being strapped to a crazed rocked and landing on Mars, but I digress).

Maybe the software you produce or the service your provide is not particularly luscious, nor does it give users the rush of being strapped to a crazed rocket, but if it is a highly useful product, you can still describe it in terms that have color, flavor, and sensuality to them. Good business writing is just good writing. Its foundation is clarity, style, and an ability to paint a clear mental picture.

There are some excellent guides to proper writing. They are all certain to help you improve your grammar and vocabulary:

• *The Elements of Style* by William Strunk and E.B. White. Since 1919, this has been one of the mainstays of good English grammar and, at fewer than 100 pages, you can read it on the train to work and amaze your coworkers when you arrive. It will certainly make your writing better.

• *Eats Shoots and Leaves.* An entertaining book by Lynne Truss, a Brit who has declared war on sloppy grammar not only in publications, but also on street signs, menus, product labels, and in advertisements. Particularly good are her lessons about the way in which a sentence can be made to convey three or four different meanings just by moving the placement of a single comma. You will never look at English in the same way after reading this book.

Her observations remind me of what a very different personality—
New York Daily News columnist Jimmy Breslin—said in 1977
about the "Son of Sam" serial killer (who, while still at large, wrote a
personal letter to Breslin). Breslin said, "[He's] the only murderer I
ever heard of who knew how to use a semicolon."

• *The Chicago Manual of Style*, published by the University of
Chicago, is one of my old favorites and the book that I used daily as
a reporter. It is comprehensive and answers most of the vexing style
questions that any businessperson or reporter could ask. First
published in 1906, the CMS is an excellent resource.

The ability to explain a concept, product, or service on paper so the
reader can understand your exact meaning is vitally important to
your public relations efforts and ultimate visibility. Even if you have
spent your entire career steeped in industry jargon, you still can
teach yourself to communicate in a way that anyone can understand.
That is the beginning of good public relations.

A Few Good Men and Women

I had an opportunity to work closely with large groups of U.S.
Marine Corps officers at Camp LeJeune, NC, Camp Pendleton, CA,
and in other parts of the country as part of a national
communications campaign. They ranged in rank from second
lieutenants to major generals. They were all a pleasure to know and
work with. The written plan we were creating was supposed to be
free of jargon, understandable by Marines and civilians alike.

But, like all professionals—in medicine, law, government,
education, technology, and science, just to name a few—the
Marines, whether writing or speaking, constantly fell back on the
jargon shortcuts they knew best. They even did so when addressing a
group of civilians like myself who were unfamiliar with Marine
acronyms and slang (I served in the Army but even that did not
prepare me for USMC jargon).

Once they had revised their writing a few times, they realized that they could communicate to their audiences, including fellow Marines, more clearly in plain English, they ejected the jargon, and their written work improved.

The Legend of Joe and Sam

Getting out of the jargon rut just takes practice. Here, for example, is a paragraph taken verbatim from a government-agency memo found on the web. I have only changed the name of the agency and its department to "Joe" and "Sam."

Version 1:

"During the course of the fiscal year, Joe audits Sam's programs, systems and operations. Joe then recommends improvements to management based on [his] findings. Sam's management may or may agree with the audit's findings and/or recommendations. An agreement is reached during the management decisions process. If management agrees with the recommendation, a written plan for correction action with the target completion date is developed and submitted to Joe for his concurrence. If both Joe and management agree that the proposed corrective action will correct the situation, management decision then is achieved for that recommendation. Once management decision is reached for each recommendation in the audit, that audit is considered resolved. Audit follow-up ensures that prompt and responsive action is taken once management decisions are reached on recommendations contained in final audit reports. Sam's Office of the Chief Financial Officer (OCFO) oversees audit follow-up for Sam. An audit remains open until all corrective actions for each recommendation are completed. As agencies complete planned corrective actions and submit closure documentation, OCFO reviews it for sufficiency and determines if final action is completed."

Did you make it through the whole paragraph? After reading it three or four times, I got it, but it was tough going. There are easier ways to convey the ideas in the paragraph above. Here is one:

Version 2:

"During the fiscal year, Joe audits Sam's programs, systems, and operations. Joe then makes recommendations to management based on his findings. Management's opinion is considered final. Sam's chief financial officer
then oversees an audit to ensure that Sam makes the changes."

Further simplified:

Version 3:

"Joe audits Sam's work. If Sam needs to change something, management decides which changes he should make. Sam's CFO then ensures that he makes the changes."

Version 4:

"I am Sam. Sam I am. I do not like audits, green eggs, and ham."

OK, maybe that's too much clarity. Laugh if you want, but Theodore Seuss got rich taking topical themes and simple language and turning them into memorable children's stories. But we'll stick with Version 2. It gets the point across without a lot of extra words, a passive voice, and doublespeak.

Try it yourself. Take something you have written. Simplify it. Now, simplify it again. Here are some guidelines:

• Put the most important information up top.

• Make every word count, while maintaining the meaning and context of the piece.

• Replace each bit of jargon with one or more plain-English words.

• Change a passive voice to an active one. Change "Charlie's contract was edited by Peter" to "Peter edited Charlie's contract."

• Read it aloud to see if it makes sense.

• Try it out on an outsider and see if he or she understands it.

There's No 'I' in Team But "Aaaaarrg" in Jargon

Every group has its own jargon and clichés and it would be impossible to cover the list of even a few occupations, avocations, or interests. But we need to be able to recognize jargon and clichés and cut them out of our writing. What is a cliché?

It reminds me of what Supreme Court Justice Potter Stewart once said about pornography: "I can't define it, but I know it when I see it." If you can't spot jargon, just watch one of the TV medical dramas; they are full of jargon from the opening theme to the closing credits. Their reasons? Using doctor speak lends an air of authority to the TV characters. After all, they are doctors giving orders to other doctors and nurses. Stat!

Attack of the Monster Clichés:

No discussion about business writing would be complete without including clichés. Clichés are like spies lurking in our copy (that was a cliché), often unrecognizable from the rest of our writing. We use them so often that they become part of the language. They're slang expressions that, at first, seem clever and descriptive, but after a few repeats, they become stale and, finally, they attack our communication.

When you see clichés in your writing, take them out and substitute plain English words that convey the same meaning and your writing will become brighter and more readable. Here are some examples of hackneyed business clichés that are still in use (and more reader-friendly replacements in plain English):

* No brainer (easy)
* Brainchild (invention, idea)
* Brain dump (briefing)
* Pick your brain (get your advice)
* At the end of the day (ultimately)

* The perfect storm of...(the right conditions for; a bad combination)
* Drill down (look for more detail)
* Granular (more detailed)
* Take it offline (talk after the meeting)
* Touch base (contact)
* Whether or not (just use "whether." the "not" is always implied)
* Best of breed (most successful)
* Rock Star (Springsteen and Elvis Costello are. Elon Musk and Warren Buffet -brilliant and rich as they may be -are not).
* Get my head around (understand)
* Close the loop (tell everyone involved)
* Low-hanging fruit (easiest to accomplish)
* Push the envelope (exceed limits)
* Win-Win (mutually beneficial)
* On the same page (agree)
* Future plans (just "plans" ALL plans are future)
* Task force (working group)
* Drink the Kool-Aid (this refers to a 1978 mass suicide; retire it)
* Currently (present tense is always implied unless you say otherwise)
* Leading or cutting edge (innovative)
* Mission critical (essential)
* Crunch time (near deadline)
* On their radar screen (we have their attention)
* Slam dunk (see "No brainer")
* If you build it, they will come (there is demand)
* Our perennial favorite, however, remains "The Paradigm Shift."

Drill Down, Get Granular

Imagine Getting a Memo Like This One: "Getting this committee to think outside the box is like herding cats. We need to strike while the iron is hot and adopt a new paradigm that will enable us to pick the low-hanging fruit. It's a no-brainer. Let's get better research—drill down and get information that is more granular so we're not flying by the seat of our pants. Let's put our heads together tomorrow at 11:00 and come up with a game plan. But be warned: There is no silver bullet."

The syntax in that paragraph is so poor that any metaphor I use to describe it would only add to your misery. It is impossible to read without rolling your eyes. With little effort, it could be rewritten like this:

"Just because we have always done things a certain way does not mean we can't look at this issue with a fresh perspective. It is hard to get the whole committee working on the issue, but we must. A new way of conducting business, I believe, will enable us to keep our current customers while winning new ones. Let's get good, detailed market research and use it to come up with some alternatives. We'll meet tomorrow at 11:00 to discuss this.

Worksheet: Clearer Writing

Which of our communications tools could use a rewrite to make them clearer and more concise? How should we revise each one?

1.

2.

3.

4.

5.

6.

7.

Write and Send Effective Press Releases

"If I am to speak 10 minutes, I need a week for preparation; if 15 minutes, three days; if half an hour, two days; if an hour, I am ready now." --
Woodrow Wilson

Chapter Summary: Top 10 Rules for Sending Press Releases; press release templates you can use to create your own.

1. Create a media list carefully and send only to reporters who really will be interested.
2. Use the right format to write your press release (see below).
3. Tie your news to a hot trend or timely topic.
4. Write releases in newspaper style, with the main news on top.
5. Be concise. About 400 words is optimal. Never more than 1½ pages, single-spaced.
6. Correct spelling and grammatical errors and get rid of jargon.

7. Include no more than two quotes; make them informative.
8. List a contact person with email address and cell number.
9. Don't limit your targets to reporters. Send releases to all of your contacts.
10. Follow up with reporters after you send out your release.

Is the Press Release Dead?

Every couple of years someone announces that the press release is dead. Come to think of it, I may have read that in a press release. But anyway, it's not true. The press release lives on because it is nothing more than a written format in which to send information to any audience including, of course, the press. Whether you send it by email, tweet, text, or have a messenger in a gorilla suit with balloons deliver it, a press release is just a convenient way to organize information. The means by which you send information does not diminish the fact that it still must be organized in such a way that makes it clearly understood.

The real change in the nature of the press release is the fact that today, using Internet tools, you can land a press release in the inboxes of tens of thousands of journalists in the time it takes you to read this sentence. That's also the problem. Blanketing the press with releases—especially those that contain little or no news—is of no use to senders or recipients. The same goes for similarly deficient emails, phone calls, blogs, press kits, fact sheets, and faxes. There is a lot of fluff out there.

When I was a reporter at U.S. News & World Report, I kept a box full of press kits for use in teaching a public relations course. What made some of these kits so remarkable was that, despite their beautiful four-color printing, fancy artwork, slick paper, and cost, so many of them contained no news—nothing that I could actually use to write a story.

No reporter will hunt through page after page of a press release or press kit (or anywhere on your website for that matter) searching for news. The sender's return on investment: zero. Organizations churn out a huge number of news-free releases every day, which are sent blindly to reporters and editors by email. No wonder reporters get so frustrated searching their inboxes!

Sending Press Releases is a Tactic, Not a Strategy

Sending press releases is not a public relations strategy. It is just one of the tactical tools at your disposal. Sending releases is similar to planting seeds in the ground. With enough attention, water, sunlight, and, yes, sometimes a touch of organic fertilizer – if you catch my drift -- it will sprout into a stout and healthy plant. But it takes some tending.

Tap Out a Steady Drumbeat of Announcements

How often should you send releases? Only when you have news, of course. But, it does not always have to be major news. Send out a fairly regular "drumbeat" of press releases even if you have routine announcements, so the name of your organization will stay in front of your audiences. This is especially important as a way to keep your name as high as possible in web searches. Press releases can be effective in announcing a number of
newsworthy developments or activities. Among them:

• A new product or service

• An event

• The viewpoint of a person or organization on a particular issue in the news

• The results of a survey

• Recognition of a trend in your industry

• A significant speech by your CEO

• A partnership between two companies

- The sale or purchase of a company

- A program designed to accomplish a specific goal

- New laws or regulations

- Personnel changes

- The winning of a new contract or other work

The trick here is to pick the right reporters. Don't send your paper's city desk an announcement about a new executive at your company, for example. That goes to the business page or, even better, to the editor who handles the column about promotions.

How to Build a Great Press Release

A press release gives reporters and editors enough information to:

- Write a short article word-for-word from the release

- Use the facts in the release to write their own story

- Understand a topic/issue/product well enough decide whether they are interested enough to write a story at all.

Two Rules for Writing A Press Release:

• The five-second rule: Can anyone pick up your release and, in five seconds or fewer, determine exactly what the news value is? That's about all of the time a reporter is going to spend on your release before he or she decides to keep or dump it.

• Next, put yourself in the reporter's place and ask yourself, "Could I write a story based on this information?"

There is no single best way to write a press release, but effective press releases generally follow a proven formula. Write your release as you'd want to see it in the paper. Some newspapers—particularly smaller ones— will run a press release exactly as written.

Here are Components Of an Effective Press Release:

No attachments: paste the text of your news release directly into an email. Most reporters won't open an attachment because it is too time consuming and it increases the chance of downloading a virus. Years ago, it was important to format releases double-spaced so editors could make changes right on the printed press release itself. Today, most releases are read online so it makes little difference to editors whether they are single or double-spaced. Single spacing takes less room and is now the preferred format.

Length: About 400 words is optimal for a press release. In any case, a release should never be more than a page and a half, single-spaced.

E-mail Subject Line: Since most press releases today go out over the Internet, it is critically important that your email subject line be compelling. Just like the rest of us, reporters will read or delete emails based solely on the subject line. Be sure to include the name of the sending organization and some key words that will turn up when people do a search on that subject.

• Avoid subject lines like: "News from XYZ Co."
• Opt instead for: "XYZ Co. Announces Six Services That Save Time for Business Travelers."
• Or even better: "XYZ Co.'s 'AirGo' Helps Cut Business Travelers' Airport Waits in Half."

Avoid phrases that will almost surely get caught in spam filters and discarded. These include "sell," "buy," a 1-800 phone number, "deal" or "wealth," just to name a few examples. Want more examples? Look in the spam folder in your own inbox.

Contact Information: List the name, email address, and cell phone number of a contact who can be reached at any time to provide information or who can track down an expert to interview.

"For Immediate Release" and "Embargo" Press releases traditionally have included the phrase "For Immediate Release" somewhere near the top of the page. This is unnecessary. Reporters assume that unless it is marked otherwise, the news is fair game to publish now.

Embargo or No Embargo

What if you have a complex announcement, you want to get the information to reporters so they can analyze and digest it, but you don't want them to publish it until a specific day in the near future? At the top of the release, write: "Embargoed for Release on DATE and TIME. Don't do this unless it is really necessary.

Keep in mind that if you distribute an embargoed release far and wide, one or more reporters may not notice the embargo instructions. Once it is published, it is public information and other reporters can simply quote the publication that broke the embargo. Hold on to your release until you can make it public or speak with each reporter you are sending it to and make sure they understand and agree to the embargo.

Headline: Your headline might be the same as your email subject line and, for the same reasons, it should be compelling, colorful, and descriptive, and include key words that will pop up in web searches on the appropriate topic. A headline should be able to stand on its own as a news item.

Forget headlines like "XYZ Association to Hold Annual Meeting in Orlando."

Try instead for a news headline: "Medical Treatment of Children in Developing Countries to be Focus of 25th Annual XYZ Association Meeting." If writing for the web, put the head in the subject line and make it short enough to read on a smartphone. The headline above, then, might be: "Medical Conference to Focus on Children in Developing World." A subhead might read: "7,000 medical professionals from 35 countries to create four-year campaign to meet needs of world's most vulnerable population."

My pet peeve is the über-cliché headline. If a meeting is being held in New Orleans, for example, you can bet that the release (and the name of the conference) will read "...and All That Jazz." If it has anything to do with canines, you can bet that something or someone is "Going to the Dogs." More about that back in Chapter 5 on the subject of clichés.

Use Newspaper Style

Lead Paragraph: Make it easy for the reporter. Write your release in newspaper style— important news in the headline and first paragraph because that's all most reporters will bother to read. The head, subhead, and the lead paragraph should answer the question "Why would this be of interest to your readers?" If it is an event, will there be any famous or at least notable speakers? Will there be "real people"— non-celebs who can provide personal insight into an issue? In the case of the medical meeting above, perhaps parents of children from developing countries affected by a lack of good medical treatment. How about doctors or nurses? Pharmaceutical company executives? Advocates? Just tell me why, as a reporter, I should schlep 1,000 miles—or even cross the street—to cover this event.

Secondary Paragraphs: Provide enough background to give context to the news. Give enough detail in case a reporter does not have time to do interviews and wants to do a short item based only on what was in the press release.

Quote(s): Quotes rarely get picked up unless they are actually newsworthy. Here is a quote, for our hypothetical example above, that could actually end up in a news story: "Thousands of children worldwide get ill from diseases for which we already have effective medicines," said Dr. Joe Jones, dean of the XYZ University Medical School. "Helping these children is as much about getting supplies quickly to where they are needed as it is about the science of creating effective medications themselves."

Quotes should come from people who are knowledgeable about the subject at hand, not necessarily the president of a company. Use no more than two quotes even if there are a half-dozen organizations involved in an announcement. More than two makes it appear – accurately --- that people involved in the announcement are elbowing each other for attention.

Organization ID or Boilerplate: (See Chapter 4 on creating this paragraph as part of your message document) Include it at the bottom of all releases to ensure that reporters understand what your organization does. This is similar to the "About XYZ" paragraph in the press release examples below.

Tailor Announcements to Your Audiences

You may need two or three versions of your press release. For example, if your company just launched a new piece of medical-related equipment, you might write a release for general press, and then others for one or two of the following: medical-engineering journals, health writers, seniors publications, technology magazines, and lifestyle publications.

Again, the format of a press release is pretty straightforward. Save your creativity for the content. On the next five pages are templates you can use to create your own press releases.

Worksheet: Press Release Schedule

Potential Press Releases to Send (see Chapter 9 for story ideas)

Month _____

- **Topic:** _____

- **Topic:** _____

- **Topic:** _____

Month _____

- **Topic:** _____

- **Topic:** _____

- **Topic:** _____

Month _____

- **Topic:** _____

- **Topic:** _____

- **Topic:** _____

Month _____

- **Topic:** _____

- **Topic:** _____

- **Topic:** _____

Template for press release on new client, new product or an improved product

News

Contact:
Leslie Smith
Phone, Email

Hartsfield Atlanta International Airport Picks XYZ Co. to Improve Flight Operations

Anywhere, Maryland - July 9, YEAR - XYZ Organization Inc., a provider of Internet-based real-time flight tracking information, reporting and display products, is helping to smooth airfield operations and improve the travel experience at the nation's busiest air travel hub -- Hartsfield Atlanta International -- the airport and XYZ announced today.

Hartsfield reports that since it began using the XYZ Organization Inc. software platform Highflier, it has seen marked improvement in its ability to track flight delays, airfield usage and demand, runway and taxiway traffic and other critical activities. (You can add more detail here).

Quote from the airport's primary user of Highflier product

About XYZ Co.
The organization ID paragraph. (See Chapter 4 on Messsages – this is the "Company ID" paragraph)

Template for press release on new product

News

Contact:
Leslie Smith
Phone, Email

XYZ Organization Inc's SavesaLottaGas Cuts as Much as 30% of Fuel and Other Delivery Costs

Anywhere, California - July 9, YEAR -- With fuel prices at record highs, some companies providing delivery services are still saving tens of thousands of dollars in delivery expenses–as much as 30 percent of their costs of fuel, mileage and manpower. They do this by using a new product called SavesaLottaGas, a map-based software system that turns hours of route planning into minutes.

Results can be dramatic- cutting route planning time by as much as 75 percent. (Add more info about the service here)

In addition to route planning, SavesaLottaGas also includes other major benefits: *List the major benefits here in bulleted form:*

Quote from SavesaLottaGas customer about specific ways in which product has saved the company time, money and other resources.

About XYZ Co.
The organization ID paragraph. (See Chapter 4 on Messsages – this is the "Company ID" paragraph)

Template for press release announcing new staff member

News

Contact:
Leslie Smith
Phone, Email

National Marketing Award Winner Joan Smith
Named XYZ VP of Communication

Anywhere, Texas - July 9, YEAR - XYZ Organization Inc., a provider of accounting software for higher education institutions, today announced the appointment of Joan Smith as vice president of marketing.

With 20 years of experience in marketing, product development, business development and general management, Smith will be responsible for setting XYZ's marketing strategy.

Quote from a company executive.

Prior to joining XYZ, Smith served as vice president of marketing for ABC, a premier business and consulting firm, where she was responsible for developing and driving strategic growth initiatives to support ABC's education, health, and information and communications technology clients.

About XYZ Co.
The organization ID paragraph. (See Chapter 4 on Messsages – this is the "Company ID" paragraph)

Template for press release announcing multiple staff or board members

News

Contact:
Leslie Smith
Phone, Email

XYZ Organization Inc., Names Three New Members to Its Board of Directors

Anywhere, Michigan–July 9, YEAR–XYZ Organization Inc., a company that manufactures some of the world's most innovative industrial products, today announced that it has named three new members to its 12-person board of directors.

The directors include two renowned inventors, Edison J. Thomas and Fulton T. Roberts as well as Sarah Brown, CEO of the nation's largest tool and die maker ABCD Company. They replace Joe Jones, June Smith and Bill Brown.

Quote from CEO about the effect that the new members of the board will have on the company and its ability to serve customers.

Here, include a 3-4-sentence mini-bio on each new board member

About XYZ Co.
The organization ID paragraph. (See Chapter 4 on Messsages – this is the "Company ID" paragraph)

Template for press release on organizational award

News

Contact:
Leslie Smith
Phone, Email

CoolCompany Magazine Ranks XYZ Organization Inc. Among 'Real Hot 100' Companies

Anywhere, New York–July 9, YEAR–XYZ Organization Inc., an information technology professional services company, today announced that CoolCompany Magazine has named it a "Real Hot l00" company. CoolCompany's Fast growth 100 ranks U.S. companies by revenue growth. Rankings are based on revenue increases over the past three years.

XYZ's ranking is the result of two-year growth from $XX million in YEAR to more than $X.X million in YEAR – more than 50%

List 3-4 areas in which XYZ has grown the most and why.

Quote by CEO of XYZ

AboutXYZ
The organization ID paragraph. (See Chapter 4 on Messsages – this is the "Company ID" paragraph)

Less Is More: Build a Great Media List

Before you send out information to the press, you must first decide which reporters are most likely to be interested in your news. Then gather their names and contact information into a media list. Include reporters you'd like to build a relationship with by sending them news they can use, the names of news sources, and updates on developments in your company, your community, or your industry. Put the information into a spreadsheet or other database.

Make sure your media lists are up to date. Reporters—especially those in the early stages of their careers—change jobs often. Some go to more prestigious outlets, others are downsized, rightsized, smartsized, or vaporized when advertising sales drop. Quality beats quantity here.

For each type of medium, you'll want to include:

• **Newspapers and magazines**: news and feature editors, reporters, and photo editors

• **TV:** assignment editors and news producers

• **Radio:** reporters, news directors, show hosts, bookers (who book guests on talk shows), and producers

• **Wire Services:** bureau chiefs, daybook editors

• **Online editors** of all of the above: virtually every traditional media outlet has an online version. Court the editors of these platforms by adding them to your press lists and building relationships with them.

• **Bloggers:** they can be invaluable since they tend to be passionate about their topics and have equally passionate readers. Start with the ones who are most influential in your industry.

There are a number of ways to build media lists. My favorites are those that range in cost from zero to just a bit more than zero. Let's examine three ways to create your lists:

Free and Almost Free: Try These First

Free:

• What industry publications do you read? What do your customers and prospects read? A reporter or two at each of these publications belong at the top of your media list. Look at the websites of those publications and locate their "Editorial Staff" or turn to the masthead (the list of who does what in the organization) in the publication itself. Many publications list reporters and editors along with their email addresses and phone numbers.

Pick reporters whose areas of coverage best match your industry or issue. Don't limit yourself to business reporters; contact those who cover the community, arts, health, sports, or whatever other areas might be a fit for your topic.

• At the end of a local-news broadcast, watch the credits and note the name of the assignment editors or producers. During the broadcast, note the names of reporters who cover stories that might include your organization. Also, of course, look at the station's website to see if they list reporters and assignment editors.

• Ask colleagues in sister organizations – those with a similar mission -- to share their media lists with you.

• Bloggers and other online media: as stated above, bloggers today have significant influence. Often, they get overlooked in favor of their colleagues in more traditional media. Get to know them, give them timely information and they will help you reach a broader audience.

• Google alerts: Google provides a platform in which you can list key words (such as company, product and peoples' names. You will get an email notification when those keywords appear in a media article. When you get an alert, note the name and contact information of the reporter who wrote it.

Almost Free:

• If you are exhibiting at a trade show, and you have some news to announce, call and introduce yourself to the person in charge of media relations for the convention. Ask for the list of reporters who have registered to attend the event. Most organizations will give you the list. Get permission to send out a brief email to those reporters, telling them that you have news to announce at the show, the number of your booth, a reason or two why they might want to visit the booth, and the names of experts from your organization who will attend.

Don't abuse the permission by sending out multiple emails; one will do. Identify the publications that are most important to you and call or email those reporters to set up in-person interviews at the event. If they will commit to an interview, suggest that you meet at a time when there is little else on the convention schedule. See Chapter 21 on trade shows.

• If your organization is having an event at which reporters are expected to attend, put out a sign-up list so they can provide their names and email addresses. This is kind of a chicken-egg dilemma, I know: How do you get reporters to come to an event if you don't already have a list of reporters to contact? Start with the list that you compiled yourself in the free examples above.

Not Free, But Worth the Price:

A number of services are available to help you create media lists. They can be helpful and efficient, especially if you need broader coverage than just the few publications in your community or the few trade journals in your industry. They will help you create your media lists, send your releases, and track which reporters opened up the email announcement and read it. But they are not cheap.

- **Cision** (cision.com) is probably the king of pay media list services, especially since it has bought up most of its competitors, large and small, over the years including

Bacon's and Vocus. It provides a huge platform of services that enables subscribers to research topics, write and send releases, create and store press lists (it provides access to the contact info of 1.6 million reporters) and post their content dozens of social media platforms. Annual Cision subscriptions at the time of this writing start at about $6,000. Cision bought up a service called "Help a Reporter Out," (helpareporter.com) fondly referred to as HARO, that lets you post information about yourself or others as experts in one or more topics. Reporters looking for experts post information about stories they are working on and you can respond with a pitch to have them include you in their stories. Signing up and using HARO's most basic service is free, but to get more value out of it, you need to pay.

- **Agility** is an excellent service that provides a full range of products from building press lists to tracking your press coverage. They charge based on which services you want and how many users you'll have on the account. The basics – creating press lists if you are a small company – will cost you about $3,000 per year. Like the other services, you can send press releases from inside the platform or download the lists as Excel spreadsheets.

- **Meltwater** is another very comprehensive service that enables users to reach the news media in a highly targeted manner and track success. An annual membership is about $6,000.

Sending Your Press Releases: Help!

You can enlist the help of services to help you send your press releases. They're not necessarily cheap but they are cost-effective and do a good job. All of the pay services listed above provide the ability to send press releases within their platforms. The most popular press release distribution services are PR Newswire (prnewswire.com) and Business Wire (businesswire.com).

Fees are based on how big a distribution you want and the length of your release. Both services require a small annual membership fee plus a per-release charge and can help you target your press release to the U.S., an individual state, region or industry.

PR Newswire, for example, has been around for more than 60 years. It charges to build media all print and broadcast media in the U.S. My favorite method (unless it truly is national news) is to pay for distribution to a single state. Whether you send it to the whole country or a single state, you get, at no additional cost, any categories of trade publications you want as well as thousands of e-news sites including those run by the major news media outlets.

There are many other similar services – some charge much less, some charge more. Others are free. Generally, you get what you pay for.

Also, there are press-release distribution services that specialize in reaching one or more minority groups. For example, Black PR Wire (blackprwire.com) reaches the African-American community and hispanicprwire.com (owned by PR Newswire) that reaches the Latino community.

Follow Up After You Send Your Release

Sending a press release is only the first step in turning a story pitch into a print or broadcast story. The second step—no less important—is following up. The conventional wisdom in public relations is that you should not call reporters to see if they have received your press release.

Most reporters will say they get hundreds of releases and don't want to be bothered. But in my experience, a quick follow-up call to a reporter makes your release stand out from the rest of the stack if you have real news to offer. Be judicious. Don't call to check on a release about a company manager being promoted to vice president, for example. Save the follow-up calls for releases that provide real story ideas: trends, hard news, and unusual activities.

Creating Content: Repurpose What You Already Have

"I handed in a script last year and the studio didn't change one word. The word they didn't change was on page 87." -- **comedian Steve Martin**

Chapter Summary: Create Written Materials the Easy Way

1. The information contained in one or two white papers, speeches, or other similar materials might be all you need to create news releases, byline articles, Op-Eds, and newsletters.
2. Paper press kits – if you use them at all -- need not be thick and heavy. Most information today travels over the Internet so if you are handing out a printed press kit at an event, include only the basics and put everything else in pdf form on your website.
3. Consider sending an email company newsletter but keep it short. You can create and send it cheaply and easily by using online services that provide templates.
4. Business cards are still a great communication tool. Don't skimp on them.

Well-written material is like a Thanksgiving turkey. Days after the big feast, you can make sandwiches and stew out of the leftovers. Creating marketing and press materials follows the same principle. Repurpose everything. First, it is probably good material to start with, information that one or more people took time and effort to create. Second, rewriting existing materials saves time and money, two resources that are always in short supply.

Now's the time to "go green" and recycle some of the PR, sales, or marketing language you have written for other purposes as long as you keep it all up to date. The same goes for speeches and other presentations, case studies, and position papers.

You can take portions of those materials, edit them, and create:

- News releases
- Website articles
- Fact sheets
- Letters to customers and prospects
- E-mail newsletters
- Op-Eds
- Letters to the editor
- Bylined articles for business and trade publications
- Postcards announcing products or events
- Speeches
- Product flyers

Bylined Articles: Great Way to Get Into the Media

Bylined articles are a great vehicle for raising your visibility. Create them by editing a white paper or other work into one or two 800-word how-to articles that you can submit under your byline to business journals or trade magazines, many of which accept articles from readers as long as the articles cover some aspect of doing business better, faster, or cheaper. Write about what you know best: your industry or other interests. Be careful not to come across as too promotional; publications won't run a giant, free ad for your company. They want news.

Even after the article runs, you can still get mileage out of the piece. Get reprints of the articles (obtain permission first) and use them everywhere—in press kits, proposals, pitch meetings. Mail and/or email the article to clients, prospective clients, potential partners, investors, and others you are trying to influence. Include a "thought you might be interested" note.

Know How to Write and Place OpEds

Op-Eds are opinion pieces that appear adjacent to the editorial page of most newspapers. It is a coveted space because of high readership and cache. Although some are written by experts with high visibility names, any one of us can get an Op-Ed published. It is a great way to get your opinion heard and to demonstrate your expertise on a topic.

Here are some tips for writing an Op-Ed and getting it placed:

• Call or send an email to the editorial page editor of your newspaper. Ask if he or she would be interested in running an Op-Ed on the topic you want to cover. The best they will tell you is that it sounds interesting but they'll need to see it before they decide whether to run it. At least you'll know whether your topic is of possible interest.

• Write about what you know best. People who have a strong opinion, firsthand knowledge, and a unique viewpoint on an issue write the best Op-Eds. Tie your Op-Ed to a topic that is currently in the news. For example, there has been a lot of talk in the media about concussions during high school and college football games. People who might be in a good position to write an OpEd on this topic would include football coaches, players, sports doctors, parents of football players, emergency room doctors, nurses, and sports-equipment manufacturers.

• Don't try to use an Op-Ed to sell your product or service. No one wants to read about how great your company is, and editors will reject this type of writing outright. However, you can refer to experience you've had in your business as an example of your viewpoint or as proof of your expertise. Remember, your real "advertisement" on the Op-Ed page is your byline that lists your name, title, and organization.

• Get to the point quickly. State your opinion, back it up with facts and then summarize. See how long most of the Op-Eds in the paper are and follow a similar format.

Press Kits Can Never Be Too Rich or Too Thin

You may be familiar with paper press kits, the kind companies used to hand out to reporters at trade shows, during interviews, and send with press releases. Years ago, before the web, it was necessary to stuff press kits full of sales brochures, press releases, company-capability books and other materials.

Today, it's all done by email or social media and posted on a "Press" page on websites. If you do put together a paper press kit – maybe for a table in the pressroom at a convention – it's not necessary to make it fancy unless you are trying to portray a fancy image— jewelry, luxury cars, or an art gallery, for example. Even then, most reporters throw away fancy folders and just staple together the innards. In any case, I prefer plainer news materials because they look more immediate and timely. Make your press kit rich with information but as light as possible on the paper side.

Press kits should include:

• A fact sheet about your organization

• The most recent press release—the one you are pitching now, hoping to get a story—and perhaps your last two or three releases

• A page of short bios of people available to be interviewed

• A Q&A about your organization, products, and services

• One or two product sheets if they pertain to the latest news you are pitching

• All of the above in pdf. form on your website so reporters can download all information

Make Your web Site a Destination

Articles and books about creating good websites abound. Here we'll just explore the idea of making a good website a magnet for all of your audiences—a destination where they can learn and exchange ideas. Unless you are doing actual commerce on a website—that is, providing products and taking in money —your site need not be technically complex. But it should be loaded with helpful information, easy to use, and attractive. Spend the extra dollars to have a professional design it, if possible.

A good website should provide two functions. The first should be to tell potential clients about your organization and what you can do for them (make sure your messages drive this function). The second should be to make it a "destination" site for anyone interested in a particular topic.

A destination website is one that is comprehensive and authoritative. It is a site that people go to for information, even if they don't yet know or even care much about the organization that runs it. Begin by including white papers, fact sheets, and links to articles and blogs. Expand it to include a well-organized list of other websites that provide good information.

Start by including white papers, fact sheets, and links to articles and blogs. Expand it to include a well-organized list of other websites that provide good industry information. If you have a landscape service, for example, post a calendar on which annuals to plant each season, an article on how to save water, a piece on which plants attract butterflies, an item on how to keep deer from eating shrubs, and other interesting information.

Ask your local garden club to write the articles and give them byline credit. Provide links to national, state, and local botanical and agricultural sites. Create an online Q&A section. Explain the differences between the common varieties of cherry, dogwood, and maple trees. Feature photos of your best landscaping work and include testimonials from happy customers. Every page of a good website should tell or imply: "Here is what we can do for you" and "We are experts; hiring us will make your life better in some way."

The E-mail Newsletter: Information vs. Spam

One of the most misunderstood forms of communication is the email newsletter. At worst, it is another long, tedious, self-serving email— spam— that does more harm than good. *Done right, it can be helpful to the recipient and a great way for the sender to stay in front of potential customers and other important audiences.*

An email newsletter can be as plain as an email or as fancy as anything you can create on the web. You can make your own newsletter, complete with attractive graphics and formatting without much effort or expense.

There are a number of companies that provide template online newsletters (you can just cut and paste your information and photos into various boxes in preformatted newsletters on their websites) and they can store your various mailing lists as well as past newsletters. Some will even provide a report of how many people opened your newsletter each time you send one. You simply create your newsletter, build one or more address lists on the site, pick the address lists you want to send to, and hit "send." I recommend this method as a way to get the best newsletter at the least cost. Try Constant Contact or Mail Chimp for starters. They charge based on the number of contacts in your database. Plan on spending a couple of hours to create your first newsletter. For your next newsletters, you can copy the previous one with a single mouse click and then just substitute your new article(s) and other content for the old stuff.

A Good Email Newsletter Should Be:

• **Informative.** I am a big believer in giving away information. No one is going to become a competitor or take away your clients just because they read a 500-word newsletter. Don't be coy; provide information that is timely, helpful, practical and easy to digest. Show readers you are an expert. Make your email newsletter on target for the intended audience. A thinly disguised ad with no valuable information is spam.

• **Compelling**. Start with the subject line of the email that contains your newsletter. Make it a great headline that lets the reader know that the newsletter includes good, helpful information.

• **Blissfully short**. Long emails are rarely read. If they are not deleted immediately, they will be stashed away with the intention of reading later and then deleted. Short means an article of 500 words or fewer. You can use the same top paragraph (an explanation of why you are receiving this email) and the same bottom paragraph (your ID or boilerplate paragraph) each time, and just change the middle to reflect your new information in the form of an article. Once people see that they can read your newsletters in a minute or two, they will be much more likely to open them.

• **Comprehensive.** If your email newsletter includes notices of meetings, membership lists, an archive of past articles, links to other industry sites, and other useful information, it is obviously bound to be longer than 500 words. But ask yourself this: If you were the recipient, would you welcome this newsletter? Better yet, every six months, ask your audience for their opinions on your newsletter.

• **Infrequent**. Monthly is optimal about as frequent as most people want. That's just enough to keep you and your contact information top-of-mind when someone needs your type of product or service. Any more frequent and it had better be extremely short (or a blog that is very targeted, personal and sought after by subscribers).

• **Graphically attractive**. This depends on your audience. If you are a graphic designer, architect, artist, photographer, interior designer or other visual-arts professional, you probably want to opt for a newsletter that is a real showcase. Otherwise, a more modest newsletter will do.

• **Invited into the recipient's mailbox**. Always provide an opt-out method, but also make it easy for recipients to share the email with friends by including a "forward" box.

Article Marketing Can Increase Your Visibility.

Do a search on your company name. How many entries do you find? Want to raise that number into the hundreds of thousands? It's fairly easy. It's also yet another use for those articles you wrote in the earlier part of this chapter. Article marketing is, by far, one of my favorite—and one of the most powerful—ways to increase visibility. It is also very easy once you learn the basics.

Here's how it works to raise your visibility: You post articles on 10 or 12 of the thousands of topic-related websites that are looking for fresh, original articles to provide to their visitors. Industry sites link to them and, within a few weeks, your articles and name are appearing all over the place as an expert.

It is a great arrangement. You are providing the sites with free information and they, in turn, are giving you free publicity and more listings on web search results. With just a few articles, the number of mentions of you and/or your organization on the web can go from just a few to hundreds of thousands in a matter of weeks.

Here's How You Do It:

• Search on the web for articles in your industry. As you scroll down through the search results, find sites that feature articles on your topic of expertise. Open them up and see if they accept article submissions. Start with about a half-dozen sites. The best sites for you will be those that deal directly with your industry, perhaps even associations to which you belong. Or, try these three general business-article sites for starters: ezinearticles.com and articlealley.com.

• Here is the easiest part: Simply paste your articles (about 500-1,000 words is standard) into online forms that the sites have provided for that purpose. Generally there are blank spaces for your name, the title of your article, a summary of the article, the full text itself, and—most important for you—a place for a short paragraph about you, the author.

• The cardinal rule of article marketing is this: Post real articles, not ads cleverly disguised as articles. Sites won't accept the latter. Provide real value to the reader and save your "ad" for the paragraph at the bottom that lists your name, company, and contact information.

Should You Use Video News Releases?

Video News Releases (VNRs)—video versions of press releases— have been around for a long time, and they are still viable media tools -- even more so now that YouTube has grown wildly. They comprise video snippets that make it easy for TV stations to run stories because reporters then don't have to go out and shoot all of the video themselves (more on that in Chapter 8). Post them on your website, YouTube channel and link them up via all of your social media platforms.

VNRs have become controversial in recent years because organizations sometimes produce them to look exactly like real TV news segments (with on-air "reporters"), when they are, in fact, advocacy pieces or commercials for the organizations that paid for them. However, if you have a new product, for example, that you think would make a good TV story, by all means consider providing a VNR, but be mindful of a few rules:

- If you have an on-air personality explaining the product, make sure she identifies herself as someone in your organization and does not imply that she is a reporter. Or, just have a person narrate the story as a voice-over without being seen onscreen. Still, anyone who appears on screen or as a voice-over should identify himself or herself properly unless it is obvious that they are a paid spokesperson (i.e, wearing your company logo shirt).

- You will also want to provide background video that TV producers can use to intermix with the video they shoot. This is called "B-Roll." If a producer is doing a story on your new product, they may want to cut to a quick shot of the front of your building, shots of the product being demonstrated, being sold in a store, and being made in a factory, if possible. Companies post B-Roll on their websites so media outlets can readily access them day or night. Otherwise, you can provide it on the video news releases that you distribute.

The Often-Underestimated Business Card

Even with the arsenal of other communication tools at our disposal—both traditional and web-related—one of my favorite means of communication remains a humble little paper rectangle. Yep, I'm talking about the lowly and often-underestimated business card. A pet peeve: I still see cards that say absolutely nothing about what the person does! What services do they provide? A week later, I toss the card because I can't remember the person or what they told me about their business.

Here Are A Few Guidelines:

• **Spend as much as necessary to have cards look great.** Get your cards made by a professional printer or online vendor in four colors on heavy coated or non-coated paper stock. A card should feel as good as it looks. Even if you are a small company, your card can look as important as those given out by Fortune 500 execs.

• **Don't use cards that you print yourself on your computer.** Although they have improved a bit over the years, they still feel and look flimsy. If your budget is tight, go to one of the office-supply chains. They offer while-you-wait business cards that look pretty good and are inexpensive. Still, they don't compare in "feel" to professionally produced cards. A better bet might be the online sites in which you can design and order business cards. The options they offer are almost limitless. Try vistaprint.com or moo.com.

• **Most important: in addition to your contact information, make sure your card says what you do!** Make it easy for people to remember what you do if they forget your name. Even if your title is "vice president," make sure there is a line on your card that says "web design firm," or "Certified Financial Planner," or "We write proposals that win contracts." Remember, they want to know how you can help them succeed.

• **Printing on the back of the card is not necessary.** I've had cards for weeks, even months, before I noticed that there was anything on the back. In fact, have your cards made uncoated on the back so you can write on them with any type of pen. But, if you do have a product or service that you want to feature on the back of the card, make it as professional-looking as the front. And, when you hand them out, remember to point out to the recipient that there is information on the back. One trick to make sure people notice the back: Dog-ear one corner of the card before you hand it out so the recipient can see that there is something on the back.

• **Unless you are in the creative arts or want to portray an image that is a bit offbeat, stick to the standard-sized card and don't make it out of anything but paper.** An oversized card or one printed on clear plastic is not likely to be kept any longer than a paper card. Odd cards are just not that novel any more.

On-Hold Messages: Someone Else's Taste in Music?

What do your callers hear when your receptionist places them on hold as they wait to be connected to a staff member? Elevator music? A local radio station? My preference, as a caller, is dead silence so I can work on other things while on hold. But, if your business lends itself to using that time to promote your company, do it. On-hold messages are a great place to put useful information (rather than driving callers crazy with slick-sounding pitches that sound like QVC). It's an opportunity, again, to demonstrate your expertise.

Put together a script that hits on your main message points. Make your recording sound like a radio story that brags about your latest products or services. To keep it interesting, record a new one at least monthly. Unless you have a staffer with a broadcast-worthy voice, hire a professional announcer to record your on-hold message so it gives callers the impression they are reaching a large company even if you are just an office of three.

Worksheet: Written Materials to Repurpose

Which existing written items such as white papers, speeches and product descriptions do we already have that we could repurpose for the website, press releases, articles, etc.

Item _____

- **Repurpose to create a:** _____

- **Repurpose to create a:** _____

Item _____

- **Repurpose to create a:** _____

- **Repurpose to create a:** _____

Item _____

- **Repurpose to create a:** _____

- **Repurpose to create a:** _____

Item _____

- **Repurpose to create a:** _____

- **Repurpose to create a:** _____

Using Social Media and Other Weapons of Mass Communications

"Like almost everyone who uses email, I receive a ton of spam every day.
Much of it offers to help me get out of debt or get rich quick.
It would be funny if it weren't so exciting." -- **Bill Gates**

Chapter Summary: Blogging Is the Best Way to Break into New Media

1. Before you start blogging, Facebooking, tweeting, podcasting, or using other social media, make sure you have your communication basics in order.
2. Blogging is probably the best way to break into social media.
3. From a PR standpoint, the objective is to get your writing out on the web and linked to other sites.
4."Google" your own organization's name to see what blogs and other postings say about you.
5. Mobile marketing—using a cell phone-friendly platform as your

primary outreach tool is here in a big way.

The Paper Vanishing Act

If you came of age before the emergence of personal computers –
and certainly before social media and cloud storage -- you know how
daunting a mountain of paper was to live with.

When I was young, in the U.S. Army and stationed in the Panama
Canal Zone, I worked in a public affairs office that was stacked to
the ceiling with papers. One February afternoon, we were told that,
in a week, our office was to be inspected by visiting stateside
commanders. (Pentagon brass always chose winter to come do their
base inspections. Average temperature in Washington: 30s, average
in Panama: 80s) We could not legally throw out or shred documents
without inspecting them because many were "official." Our senior
officer went into a panic because we had no place on the entire base
in which store the mountain of papers.

Fortunately, every Army unit seems to have a wily sergeant or two
who can make anything happen as if by magic, from procuring a
jeep for the night to acquiring 200 cans of red paint. So did we. Our
sergeant calmly made a phone call and then told us to box everything
up. He would take care of it. Over the next three days we filled
hundreds of boxes with tons of paper. Then one morning we came
into the office and everything was gone. Poof!

The sergeant had called an old buddy at the base postal facility after
sticking a label on each box with *our own office as the addressee.* A
fleet of green mail trucks took away the boxes. A week after the
inspection—which we passed—the trucks came back to deliver the
boxes that we had mailed to ourselves!

Use Your Superpowers Wisely

Facebook, Twitter, Instagram and other platforms have given us
superpowers as good as anything Marvel could have dreamed. It is
the power to push ideas -however mighty or mundane -into other

peoples' minds. It is a mighty power that should not be abused. Take food photos, for example.

Years ago, if people wanted to share a photo of their breakfast with friends, they had to take a photo of the food, have the drugstore make 500 prints, write up a caption and paste it onto the back of each photo, address and stamp all of the envelopes, insert the photo into all 500 envelopes and take the whole thing to the post office. Doing that three or four times a day, every day, was very time consuming. Thank goodness social media came along and we can share important news and photos about our eating habits .

Social media is a very powerful communications tool and should be part of the your PR strategy. If you want to be a real social media expert, there are thousands of great articles, guides, courses and videos that will help you do that. But this chapter is written with generalists in mind, those who wants to make social media a *part* of their public relations activities. It is designed to take the mystery out of the medium and help you use common sense to choose your tactics.

Do you find the whole idea of tweeting, blogging and posting to other web-based communication tools intimidating and something that everyone in the world except you seems to be latching onto? Take a deep breath and let it out slowly. We can fix that. Keep reading. First, remember that just because you can do something, does not mean that you should do all of it at the same time.

"Can vs. Should" is Not a Landmark Supreme Court Case

My neighbor has an impressive collection of professional-grade woodworking tools: circular saws, lathes, band saws, belt sanders, grinders, and drill presses. Every time I go over to his house, I tell myself that I really should buy some of that stuff because it would take my skills to a whole new level. And then I remember -- palm to forehead — I don't even *do* woodworking. Maybe I could just start with a small saw and drill and make a few birdhouses before tackling early French Renaissance furniture.

"Start-from-Zero" Best Way to Begin Using New Technology

Let's use the same "can vs. should" principle as the woodworking example above to discuss web-based tools. I suggest you not try to absorb and use everything in this chapter at once. Read through the sections, select one or two tools that sound like they make sense for you now, and give them a try. Like learning anything new— a language, a musical instrument, a new kind of software—I like to use what I call the "Start from Zero" approach. I take the techniques that I already know and use (the zero starting point) and slowly add in other techniques and tools as I need them.

Web-based communication tools provide additional ways to do what successful people in business have done for decades: create open channels of communication, conversation, and understanding between individuals in companies, communities, governments, and other organizations.

Pause at the edge of the cliff before you dive into social media. Many small-to-midsize companies are still in the throes of 1) getting their main messages together, 2) fixing their stale and outmoded websites, and 3) just starting to reach out to the news media for visibility. Get a good start on those basic steps before tackling the wonders of social media. If you are going to set up a blog to reach out to your audiences, for example, it pays to wait until you have something effective to say to them using your main messages. (See Chapter 4.)

Assuming you have the basics in good order, here is some advice on using the primary new tools of social media: blogs, social networking, podcasting, etc. If you have not yet used these tools, or you are just starting to, this section will serve to explain in plain English what they are, how they work, who should use them, and how to get started.

Because of the speed at which Internet-based tools evolve, the best place to get information about web-related tools is always on the web itself. I have listed some of the best online resources in each section.

Nothing Says "Forever" Like Embarrassing Photos

Remember that whatever you post on the web will be there for thousands of years and forever accessible by anyone including hiring managers, voters, fiancés, the news media, in-laws, children, college-admissions deans, law-enforcement officers, bosses, colleagues, investors, employees, competitors, spouses, ex-spouses, old flames, new flames, flames' friends, banks, credit bureaus, the IRS, the CIA, the NSA, DHS, AARP, PBS, CNN and the FBI. So, maybe hold off posting that photo of your face painted in your home team's colors wearing a helmet with two beer cans affixed to it.

Blog and the World Blogs with You

What it is: Of all of the new weapons of mass communication, none have been written about, talked about, and blogged about more than blogs. Short for "web logs," blogs are websites that enable you to create an online "diary" accessible by just a few people or, if you choose, the entire planet. What makes blogging so powerful is that, as bloggers read others' postings and, in turn, link their blogs to those postings, they form a quickly growing—often global— web of information.

There was a time when only a few media giants had instant access to the world audience. Now you do too, and it costs you nothing but your time and energy (no small things, granted, but you don't need a pile of money at least).

Why use it: Blogging gets you into the public "conversation" about ideas. If you are passionate about a topic, you can find numerous blogs onto which to post your opinion and have others respond. The immediacy, reach, and personal nature of blogging make it exciting. Active blogging is to communication what compound interest is to money. It expands even while you are sleeping.

Search engines are programmed to look for fresh content, so if you want your blog to get attention and rise nearer the top of searches, you'll need to update it regularly. Keeping an eye on blogs is an excellent way to monitor your industry, know what is being said about your products and services, watch your competitors, and track critical issues. There are websites that can help you find and monitor blogs.

How to get started: The best way to get started as a blogger is by reading existing blogs to get a sense of what they contain and how they are structured. Use Google's blog search function, type in a key word, and voilà, you have at your fingertips a whole list of blogs. You can then spend the rest of the day reading people's musings on any topic imaginable. Beats working!

When it comes to starting your blog you have the following options: free and self-hosted platforms. When you're starting out, free blogging platforms such as Blogger or Tumblr work just fine. The problem, however, is that every time you send out a blog post, it will have the "from" address in the form of yourname.blogspot.com or yourname.tumblr.com – a sure sign that this blog post comes from a beginner. And, Blogspot or Tumblr will own your blog name.

Self-hosted platforms allow you to choose a domain name (e.g., your organization or personal name) and you'll own the content, the name, and be in complete control. The most popular pay platform isWordpress.org. Google itself has a blogging platform.

You now need to decide what purpose your blog is going to serve—a personal journal, professional observations, political opinions? It's your space; you can write whatever you like.

You are Now a Blogger

Congratulations, you are now a blogger! You can draw attention to your site by contributingcomments to other people's blogs. Also, if yourcontent is compelling—whether it is hard news, gossip, or just interesting writing of any kind, and other bloggers link their sites to yours, prettysoon you will be part of a large network and yourexposure will increase. Be sure to put relevantkey words in the titles and content of your blogs to make it as easy as possible for search engines to find your pages.

The most dramatic use of blogs is to report breaking news. Blogs – along with Twitter, Facebook and a couple of other platforms that have users in the multi-millions worldwide -- can break news that spreads so quickly over the web that they can outstrip the ability of traditional media to keep up.

One interesting development is that traditional news outlets are incorporating information from blogs into their regular news coverage. Reporters and editors often have favorite blogs that they monitor both for news and to get the names of newsmakers they can interview.

Identify a few bloggers who are the most influential in your industry and read their blogs carefully. Treat bloggers like any other news reporters. They can be important in helping your audiences find you on the web and their reach can be enormous. Introduce yourself via email, if you like, and help them understand that you might be a good source of information. Remember, when you write something on a blog, you are entering a community. Don't just bust in and start writing.

Podcasting: Get Your Voice Out to Millions

A podcast starts out as nothing more than a digital recording. It's just a small data file like a text document or a spreadsheet. Your recording becomes a podcast once you 1) post it to a website and make it available as a file for others to download or 2) you send it by email to one or more people. The content can be virtually anything audible: a presentation, music, news reports, lectures, music, education lessons, an advertisement, an audio book, or a how-to on any topic. Recipients can download your podcast and listen to it on their iPods or other digital players, on their computers, cell phones, or other devices—anything that can play a digital recording.

Why use it: For public relations purposes, podcasts, like other social media tools, give you thechance to speak directly to your audiences with-out having the information filtered by the newsmedia. Like radio, a podcast is personal. It putsyou one-on-one with your audience; it's yourvoice in their ear. But unlike radio, listeners canaccess and listen to a particular podcast whenever they want.

Here is one way you might reach your audiences with a podcast. Let's say you send out a regular online newsletter.

Include a link to the page on your website from which visitors can download a selection of podcasts on your topic of expertise. Or, put the podcasts into the newsletter itself.

How to get started: Start by downloading podcasts that others have created. Play them on your computer or listen to them on your tablet or phone to get a sense of how they sound. They are available on the websites of well-known organizations such as National Geographic, NPR, the Smithsonian Institution, universities, media companies, and hundreds of others that are not so well known. Many individuals have become quite famous and popular through nothing but their podcast series.

To Make Your Own Podcast:

1. Remember, a podcast starts out as a digital recording saved to your computer. Plug a microphone into your computer's sound-card input. (It will be right next to the jack for your speakers) or your laptop's particular input. Then use the simple software included on most computers to record audio snippets. Save it to your desktop. (Or, get yourself a good-quality digital recorder available in most electronic or music-supply catalogs—usually less than $200 at sites like Sweetwater.com or Musiciansfriend.com.) They also sell complete kits that include a mic and desk stand, a computer interface and the software to record and edit on your laptop.

2. Post the file of your recordings on your website and let everyone know via email, blog, newsletter, or other means that it is available.

Videocasting

All of the above information about podcasting also is true of "videocasting" – creating and sending or posting videos. You can record and then post them to YouTube and then link to them from all of your social media platforms.

Frankly, one of the easiest way to create a videocast is through a Facebook account. You can jump right onto your account and run a live broadcast and record it for all of your followers to view later.

The benefits of this feature are the same as the dangers: It is Too Easy! Think carefully before you go "on the air" to all of your Facebook followers. If you want to broadcast from a frat party, go ahead, but remember that it will be available somewhere searchable online for 1,000 years – even if you delete it later.

(SEO): Getting Finches into Your Backyard

The term gets thrown around so much now that it's hardly jargon any more. I'm talking about "search-engine optimization" or SEO. If you're going to dabble in social media, so it's good to know what SEO means and how it can help you.

With virtually everything on the web searchable by Google or other browsers, a big business has emerged in helping companies rank at the top of the list in web searches. Obviously, it is a major advantage—when someone searches on the web for the ABC Widgets that you make—for you to appear toward the top of the list, ahead of your competitors, rather than buried 10 pages back where no one will find you.

People tend to buy from companies that appear among the first dozen or so entries on search lists. Search engines are programmed to look for sites that have keywords and fresh material and to bring those sites to the top of search lists.

Actually, the principle is not much different than attracting finches to your backyard. Put the right seed (thistle) in the right container (bird feeders) where they can't miss it (in a tree), and they will find you. On the web, you do this mostly by inserting keywords (thistle) on web pages (bird feeders) to make it easy for those search engines (finches) to find your backyard. When someone does a search for "chocolate gift baskets," for example, you want to make sure those three words and any others related to the topic are on your website. The trick is to ensure that as many as possible of the right keywords are embedded in your website, articles, or blog postings.

In the case of someone who makes chocolate gift baskets, keywords and phrases could also include:

• Valentine's Day gift
• Chocoholic
• Candy
• Office gift
• Workplace gift
• Mother's Day gift
• Dark chocolate
• Chocolate pretzels
• Chocolate good for your heart
• Hot chocolate

You get the idea. Although it is not too difficult to make your web postings more attractive to search engines, this is probably a good task to hire out to people who do this stuff frequently because it does require some fairly regular updating. And companies like Google keep moving the goalposts – their algorithms that control how websites are ranked and found change on a regular basis.

Mostly, it's to keep people from gaming the system – making a site come out on top even when it generates little public interest. Also, you need to know exactly where to place the keywords so they will be as accessible as possible. This can differ from one website to another. It's a pretty good investment if you want to be more visible on web searches.

I-Tube, YouTube, We All Tube.

What it is: YouTube is a site that enables anyone to post online videos of a personal and professional nature. From a business standpoint, it is a good place to post videos of your products, snippets of presentations, and other activities you'd like your customers to see.

Why use it: There are millions of YouTube videos of celebrities and regular people doing wacky things and you just have to accept that you live in that odd electronic neighborhood if you post your videos to YouTube. But, it has become an excellent place to demonstrate products and talk about services, among other things. Keep your videos short, use simple close-up shots, and lead people to your videos by linking to them from your website, your online newsletter, and other communication.

The biggest plus is that video content acts like a magnet to your website. It ranks high in SEO. From a user standpoint, there is hardly anything in the world you cannot how to do by tracking down a how-to video on YouTube – whether you want to repair an appliance or learn how to play harmonica.

How to get started: Using YouTube could not be simpler once you've recorded your videos and have them available on your computer desktop, waiting to upload. Just go to youtube.com, register, hit the button marked "UPLOAD," and follow the instructions. Once you have them posted, you can copy and paste the URL of each video into your website as a link.

Mobile Marketing: Be Ready for It

The jury is no longer out. The cell phone is becoming *the* primary web tool of choice since virtually everyone carries one around in a pocket or purse. For better or worse, "mobile marketing"—sending ads and other text messages to cell phones—is fast becoming one of the most pervasive communication techniques.

Advertisers supposedly need your permission before sending ads or other information to your cell phone but they appear anyway as do robocalls and other uninvited messages. You can give permission to companies that will send you sports scores, stock-price updates, information about product discounts, and hundreds of other bits of information. For us non-tech mortals, the thing we need to know about mobile marketing is that every website, blog, e-newsletter or other communication absolutely must be optimized to look great on a small smartphone screen. The proper term is "responsive."

Facebook and LinkedIn

What it is: You can never go broke providing new means by which people can communicate with each other. Social networking sites are places online where users create profiles of themselves and build personal networks that connect them to other users. Today, hundreds of millions of Internet users are involved in this sort of community building.

Two of the most common sites are Facebook and LinkedIn. Facebook is both personal and business – everything from cute cat photos to news from the New York Times. LinkedIn users skew more toward the business side – building a profile page and using it to connect with others in business, find a job, seek consultants, etc. Generally, in order to view someone's site, they have to invite you to do so.

Why use it: social networking sites enable long-lost friends, new acquaintances, potential customers, and business partners to find you online in a much more efficient manner than doing a general search on the web. You can narrow your search using keywords that might be in the profiles people post on the sites. For example, if you are looking for an attorney with technology industry experience in southern Florida who can help you incorporate your business, you can easily find people with those attributes by putting those key words into a LinkedIn search bar and off you go.

How to get started: Go to linkedin.com and set up an account, create a profile (with professional and personal information—whatever you are comfortable providing), and invite colleagues, friends, clients, and others (via an email generated within LinkedIn) to join your network. If they are already members of LinkedIn, they might have networks that already include a big circle of people.

Let's say you invite a dozen people to be in your network. Each of them, in turn, has a network of a dozen people and each of their contacts has a dozen more and so on. With only a few people in your immediate network, (friends, colleagues, family) you can be connected indirectly to hundreds of thousands, even millions of people.

Able to Leap Tall Buildings

This is a good time and place to consider practices that will help us keep our wits about us in this hyper-information age:

• Don't abuse friends, colleagues, or small animals with the supernatural powers that electronic communication gives you. Start with good, old-fashioned email etiquette. A good example of e-buse is the classic office email asking 30 people if they can attend a meeting at a certain time. Everyone is then compelled to hit "Reply All" in response. Well, 30 times 30 is 900 memos! Even worse, some of the email responses will be unbearably self-aggrandizing. "Sorry, I will be at the base camp of Everest," or "I have to be in Stockholm that day to accept the Nobel; can we reschedule?" Let the original sender collect all of the RSVPs and send out a confirmation count in a single email. Otherwise, we will soon run out of megabytes.

• Don't hard-wire your soul to your computer, PDA, or cell phone. Put yourself on what Timothy Ferriss, in his book The 4-Hour Workweek calls a "low-information diet." There are a number of ways to do this. Ferriss offers a number of suggestions, but I especially like this one: "Check email twice per day, once at 12:00 noon and again at 4:00, times that ensure you will have the most responses from previously sent emails." He further advises creating an auto response telling senders that you check emails only twice per day. "If they need to reach you for something urgent, it instructs, call on the phone." Makes me feel calmer just thinking about it.

Worksheet: Social Media Strategy

Which social media platforms do we want to use? How often do we want to post? What messages are most appropriate for each platform?

Platform	Frequency	Message
1. Facebook		
2. Twitter		
3. LinkedIn		
4. Instagram		
5. Snapchat		
6. Others		

Recognizing Hot Story Ideas

"Gossip is just news running ahead of itself in a red satin dress."-- **columnist Liz Smith**

Chapter Summary: How to Spot a News Story in Your Organization

1. Before you contact reporters to pitch story ideas about you or your organization, make sure you have real news to give them. Ask yourself this: If you were a reporter, could you make a story out of the information? Can you picture the story in the newspaper?
2. Your news need not be earth-shaking, just a good match for the reporter you are pitching. It might be news about a personnel change, a new product or service, or even a new client.
3. Identify a news "hook," decide which publications would be interested in your news, and then identify the right reporter at each publication.

They Ran That? I've Got a Better Story!

A newspaper is a huge hole, lined with paper, that has to be filled with gallons of ink. Given the manpower and the expense of printing up a daily paper, you'd think every story that made it into the paper would be a zinger. But there is a double whammy at work here, both due to the rise of internet news and the fact that fewer and fewer people are subscribing to newspapers and magazines.

First, with smaller budgets, the papers (and magazines) themselves are getting smaller and so is the size of the reporting staff, giving you fewer places in the paper to get your story printed. Second, papers and magazines have to compete with all of the shiny stories on the internet that come complete with video, instant updates throughout the day and links to related stories.

So, to compete, newspapers have to provide the frivolous (that's in the eye of the beholder) and the serious. In no particular order, I have just seen stories about: an otherwise normal woman who forgot the name of her street, how to take good selfies, using squash in family recipes, good places to eat in Helsinki. Certainly, there must be some space in the paper for your story, especially if it is about a great product, service, or cause that will make people's lives better in some way.

The same goes for TV. In a 30-minute newscast, only about eight minutes is devoted to hard news. The rest is commercials, weather, sports, and softer features.

Just for reference (a "baseline," if you will), here are five feature stories that, if true, would guarantee immediate coverage:

- Animal trainer teaches a dog to talk and, it turns out, the dog has a lot on his mind.
- Teenage skateboarder is "stoked" to win Nobel Peace Prize.
- Amateur astronomer receives a communiqué from a distant planet. They have received our broadcast signals and want to know why "Seinfeld" was cancelled.
- Four out of five dentists will respond to surveys on just about any topic.

- Cure for hiccups is discovered accidentally by an entire movie theater audience during first five minutes of Friday the 13th.
- An entire month passes without the arrest of a movie star for a traffic, drug, alcohol or other violation.
- Man leads a horse to water and makes him drink.

Take heart though; every organization including yours has stories that deserve press attention. While there are no guarantees on getting your story into the paper, of course, journalists are always looking for stories that have not been told before. Falling short of this kind of "man bites dog" news listed above, you can still get coverage if you learn to think like a reporter.

Just because your CEO is coming to California all the way from New York for a meeting and has time to do an interview means nothing to an LA Times reporter—unless it's an A-Lister like Bill Gates, Richard Branson or Warren Buffet. But, if you have a great story idea, and it just happens you're your CEO is an expert on the topic, that's different. Before you call a reporter, ask yourself whether the story idea you are suggesting would interest you if you were not affiliated with your company.

Here are a few guidelines on what is NOT news and what is HOT news.

Not News: Our CEO will be in town; do you want to interview him?

- Hot News: We know your beat and know that you are working on a series on XYZ. Our CEO is an expert on the subject. He will be in town in a week. Can he call or come see you? He can also give you three or four more excellent sources for your stories because he has been in the industry for 25 years.

Not News: We are having an event to celebrate our 20th anniversary.

- Hot News: Our organization was started 20 years ago as the result of discoveries X, Y, and Z that [changed peoples' lives significantly]. The 20th anniversary of those discoveries is in two months and it will be newsworthy. Speakers at our anniversary event will include a number of local and national notables such as...

Not News: We just hired a new executive.

• Hot News: We just hired a woman whose grandfather was one of the Marines in the famous flag-raising photo at Iwo Jima.
• Hot News: We just promoted a guy to partner in our law firm who was once a roadie for The Grateful Dead.
• Hot News: Our new vice president of sales and marketing more than tripled sales at [company XYZ] and has 10 guidelines for other executives who want to do the same.
• Hot News: Our new deputy CFO is 26 years old with a degree from the London School of Economics. She helped earn her way through school by writing poems for The New Yorker magazine.

Not News: We just launched a new software product that can process data quickly.

• Hot News: We just launched a new software product that will enable the FBI and police departments to share fingerprints in seconds instead of hours.
• Hot News: We just launched a new software product that 20 states already have said they will use to process state-employee pension checks, saving them millions in staff hours.

10

Story Telling is Everything!
16 Story Ideas to Attract Press

"No storyteller has ever been able to dream up anything as fantastically unlikely as what really does happen in this mad universe."
-- science fiction writer Robert Heinlein

Chapter Summary: Story Ideas Are Everywhere. Just Look for Them

Good reporters and PR people have at least one thing in common: They can come up with good story ideas, based on timely facts or events. If you want to be a great communicator, you have to be a great story teller. Here are a few ideas that your organization can use to tell your story:

- Spotlight a staff member's accomplishments
- Spotlight the story of one of your clients or other contacts

- New contract win. What does it mean? Send a release and post it on your website.
- Statement about a legislative or social issue of interest to your members. Jump on it quickly by sending out a release with your position.
- Awards: If you win a major national or industry award it may be newsworthy.
- Partnerships The most newsworthy partnerships are those you make with organizations that have high visibility.
- New members of your staff. What is the "color" in their personal and professional lives – hobbies, avocations, accomplishments, talents, family, etc.

Want to get the news media's attention? Make an emotional connection as we discussed in Chapter 1. People relate best to people. Even if your story is about, say, a new office building, the core of the story likely will include information about the people who will use it, the architect who designed it and even the people who miss the great little decades-old restaurant that it replaced.

Great stories include emotions — happiness, sadness, shock, surprise, success, faith, despair, wonder, hope, mystery, failure, and love. Your story ideas will have a much better chance of getting accepted by reporters if they have one or more of these elements. Make it personal – don't be afraid to show that you are human. Be anecdotal – have a beginning, middle and end. Have a viewpoint. Include a call to action – why are you telling me this story and what do you want me to do about it?

Great Ways to Get Press Attention

Here are 16 great ways to come up with story ideas that will get you into the newspaper, on TV, on the radio, or onto Internet news websites:

1. Commission a study or survey, the results of which will need to be of high appeal to the news outlet or outlets you want to reach. For example, if you run a restaurant, do a survey of all of your female (or male) customers for a month. Ask them "What is the sexiest dish a man (or woman) can order? " Give the results to the local paper. On a slower news day, it will make a great little feature.

Here are some quirky questions that, if they have not already been answered in a past survey, they should be:

• Do you talk to strangers? What is the most interesting thing you have learned from them?

• How often – if ever -- do you post selfies?

• How much "alone" time do you need in an average week? How much do you get?

• Who makes most of the movie selection decisions when you go to the theater?

• Does your car have a name?

• How much older than you does someone have to be for you to consider them old?

• Do you smile when you pose for photos?

• Do you decide what to wear each day more than 30 minutes in advance?

• When you're in a crowded elevator, do you stare down at your shoes or up at the floor numbers?

• Do you give change to homeless people on the street?

• What is the most you have ever paid for a coffee drink?

There are various ways to conduct informal surveys and many of them are "free."

Here are a few of the more popular basic survey platforms. Most provide basic polling for free and then offer fee-based higher-level services. One of the most popular platforms for doing surveys is surveymonkey.com. It's inexpensive and easy to use. There are many others. See Chapter 22 for more information on surveys.

2. Highlight a milestone. Does your organization have an anniversary or an accomplishment to brag about that is of significant public interest? Was yours the first company in your industry to use the internet to sell products? If so, the anniversary of the World Wide Web or your company's 10,000th sale might be a good hook for a story.

3. Create a list of trend stories in your industry, all of which could include your organization/product/issue as an example to support the subject of the articles. Match up each trend idea with an appropriate publication and reporter.

4. Tie your story to news events that are already getting high visibility. Big stories have long coattails. You might be able to provide a unique and/or local perspective to a story that is in the national news.

5. Identify newsworthy people in your organization. Get the facts (and their permission) and bring them to the attention of the news media. For example, if a member of your accounting department is an accomplished portrait painter, it may be a good story for the arts section of the newspaper. ("Painting by the Numbers" ☐ ☐I couldn't resist.)

I attended a guitar workshop and sat next to a forest ranger from the West. When someone started talking about big storms, he piped up, "I know a little something about lightning; I've been hit☐twice." Asking the obvious, I said, "What does it feel like?" He rolled his eyes, "Are you kidding? It hurts like hell!" A guitar-playing, straight-talking forest ranger who's been struck twice by lightning! Somewhere there's got to be a newspaper or magazine story looking for this guy.

6. Create a "Source List" for reporters. Pick a topic that one or more members of your organization can speak to with expertise. Provide a short written summary of each person's background and skills and include a central contact person (you?) to call to reach these experts. Distribute to reporters.

7. Write a story yourself. Write an "experts" column on a topic related to your industry. Many business publications – especially their websites or newsletters -- will accept these if they are well written, offer specific advice, and do not overtly promote you or your organization. Somewhere in your office is a white paper that you can turn into plain English, whittle down to 800 words, and submit as an article. Check first with the editor of the intended publication to determine whether he or she is interested.

8. Provide camera-ready graphics or artwork for any story idea. Make sure that any graphics are easily understood and attractive. Also, be sure to credit the name of the artist or photographer who created the work and make sure you have permission to use it. You will endear yourself to the reporter and the publication design staff for your help in dressing up the story.

9. Grab ideas from stories that have already been published. Check the websites of newspapers across the country. You may find a feature or business story idea in a paper in some other city that your local newspaper has not picked up on. Ideas can come from anywhere.

10. Shoot a "wild" photo. No, a wild photo is not one of those souvenir shots that people bring back from a Kenya safari. A wild photo is simply one that is not attached to a story—just a good photo and a caption. Newspapers carry them all the time, often on the front page. If you shoot a photo of a newsworthy event, you can package that photo with a good, descriptive caption and send it to a publication. Like anything else, if it is good enough and your timing is right, you'll have a good chance of getting it published, especially in regional or local papers that do not have large photo staffs.

Following Are A Few Things To Remember:

• **The photo.** With today's smart phones delivery time is instant. You can shoot a photo at an event, write the caption, send it to a newspaper, and you are done. Of course, the photo has to be well composed and sharp. Even outdoors (yes, even at the beach or in the snow), use flash; it removes harsh shadows from people's faces and makes them stand out from the background. Even point-and-shoot cameras have a "fill flash" setting.

Virtually all cellphones today have cameras with resolution good enough to shoot photos for the web and for paper publication -- at least for newspapers; magazines usually need higher resolution.

• **The caption.** Look at photos in your target newspaper to get an idea of the format and style. Photo captions must describe specifically what is going on in the photo with just a bit more detail than you'd find in a photo that accompanies a news story. Also, make sure you identify the people in the photo with correct names and titles.

• **Caution:** If you are sending to multiple publications, send a separate and differently composed photo to each publication. Don't send the same photo to rival newspapers. You might send one photo to a local paper and another to an industry magazine and write a different caption for each. This rule may not apply if you have a photo that is of such high news value that every newspaper would want it. In that case, contact the Associated Press or a major national publication.

11. Take video with your cell phone and post it to Twitter, Facebook and your other social media platforms. Be sure to tag important press on the post so they'll see it. Or send it to the local version of "Eyewitness News." Most local TV news stations will accept amateur videos that have high news value and are fairly well shot.

In Washington, D.C., for example, the evening news once led off with a story about a downtown bus that had burst into flames. The only video available was shot by a passerby with a smartphone. If you take such a video, call the station and ask for the news desk or assignment desk. They'll want you to either email or deliver the video to the station. Be sure to give them accurate information about its contents.

You can even use this technique to promote your product or service. Let's say you're at a trade show and someone famous tries your quirky product in a way that is humorous or unusual, make a short video. You might have something the local TV station will run.

12. Write letters to the editor of your local newspaper. People do read them and, if well-written and thoughtful, they make an impact.

13. Write and send press releases. This is certainly the most common—
and often misunderstood— method of reaching the press. See more information in Chapter 6.

14. Running an awards program can be a big newsmaker but, unless you are sure you have the staff and other resources to devote to it, I'd advise against it. Once you decide to launch an awards program, you will have to determine the entry rules, create entry and promotion materials, announce and promote the contest, appoint judges and get them to sift through entries, award the prizes, and then promote the results. Award programs can work well for larger organizations. But if you are a small company, it's probably better to hold off and use those resources elsewhere.

15. Jump into a story that is already in the works. There is also another way to get into print or on the air—get included in a story that has already been planned. But how do you know when a newspaper, magazine, or other news outlet has a story in the works? Here are a few methods—some free, others not:

The easiest way to learn about ongoing stories is simply to ask reporters you have a good working relationship with what stories they are working on. They probably won't give you much detail so as not to tip off competitors and lose the scoop, but if they think you or your company will be a good addition to the story, you'll get at least some basic information about the piece.

16. Editorial calendars. These are lists of themed magazine issues or newspaper supplements—planned months in advance by the advertising departments at publications. They are post the calendars on their website and are happy to give you the information in the hopes that you will buy and ad.

EdCals, as they are known, are designed to attract advertisers but they are a great way for you to learn what stories are planned for the coming year. Check a publication's website under "Advertising" to see its editorial calendar. This is valuable information both for editorial and advertising purposes. If you want to get numerous EdCals but don't want to go to each publication's website, a number of companies will provide those lists for a fee. They include prnewswire.com and cision.com among many others.

17. Take note of a "First of a Series" story and contact the reporter. If you and your company would fit into the series as good sources of information, contact the reporter and give him or her specific reasons why you should be included in the next installment.

18. Take note of a major event that is likely to be covered by the media. Think holidays, anniversaries, court cases, VIP visits, etc. Does your product, service or issue have a direct connection to any of these events? Use that connection as a hook to pitch your story. Know exactly which reporter you are going to call when world or national news breaks that affects you or your company. Keep the list handy.

Help a Reporter Out (HARO)

A number of services are available in which you can post information about yourself and list your qualifications as an expert in virtually any subject imaginable or even get emails from reporters looking for experts just like you. A good one is HARO (Help a Reporter Out). Just go to the site and register, listing field of expertise and a bit about yourself.

ProfNet (profnet.com) is a service of PR Newswire that enables journalists to send emails to ProfNet customers describing stories they are working on and the types of experts they are looking for as information sources. If you are a subscriber, you can respond directly to the reporters to let them know that you have the information they need.

Punchy Language for Radio

Pitch your stories to radio too. Although most radio reporters write their own scripts, they often appreciate getting copy in radio format instead of the standard news release style. Rewrite your announcement in one or two paragraphs, using short sentences and punchy language. Generally, radio spots have 1) a teaser phrase, 2) the story itself, and 3) an ending that wraps the whole thing up. Also, make sure to spell phonetically any hard-to-pronounce names or other words. For example:

"TIRED OF BEING TAILGATED ON THE HIGHWAY? WELL, SO WAS JOHN KRCZYK ("KRAW-CHICK") OF MADISON, WISCONSIN. SO, HE DECIDED TO DO SOMETHING ABOUT IT. JOHN RIGGED UP A BRIGHT SIGN ON THE BACK OF HIS PICKUP TRUCK THAT LIT UP WHEN HE PRESSED A BUTTON. IT SAYS "PLEASE STOP TAILGATING ME OR I WILL CALL THE POLICE. " DOES IT WORK? [QUOTE FROM JOHN] "OH, YEAH. MOST PEOPLE READ IT AND THEY BACK OFF PRETTY QUICKLY. BUT IT DOES MAKE SOME PEOPLE ANGRY."

Worksheet: 10 Great Story Ideas About Our Organization
(And which would make great press releases? See chapter 6)

1.

2.

3.

4.

5.

6.

7.

8.

9.

10.

11

If You Read Only One Chapter, This is the One! Learning to "Pitch" Great Story Ideas

---

"There never was a man on Earth who pitched as much as me. But the more I pitched, the stronger my arm would get." **-- baseball legend Satchel Paige**

Chapter Summary: Know How to Tell a Good Story

1. Being "on message" and knowing how to pitch a story will give you media-placement superpowers.
2. Get into the media by doing a big chunk of the reporters' work for them: providing story ideas (especially trends) and tell them why your ideas are timely.
3. Make the effort to get to know the top reporters in your industry.
4. Be a storyteller. Good stories have a beginning, middle, end and plenty of human interest.

5. Create a stunt—you can do so without spending a lot of money.
6. Forget the common wisdom about not calling reporters after you send out a press release.
7. Pitch reporters during their "off " hours.

Knowing How to Pitch Stories Will Get You into the Press

If you read only one chapter in this book, this is the one. The ability to "pitch" stories to reporters will get you more ink than a bevy of eager PR staffers singing your praises and cranking out news releases. It is THE great skill to have in raising the visibility of your organization.

Now that we've talked about "what" is newsworthy and how to recognize (or create) the news hidden inside your organization, let's explore "how" to get this information to the press in a way that will make them take notice.

What do reporters want? They want to write the same kinds of stories all of us like to read: stories with conflict, emotion, new information, trends, and, when possible, famous or at least unusual people. And they need the information within the crazy 24/7 deadlines that make up the news business today.

Look through your favorite news outlet – whether online or print. A large percentage of the items—particularly feature stories— came about because the people who are mentioned in the articles actively "pitched" the reporters. Many media stories come from ideas provided by people with a vested interest in getting the stories placed. Nothing wrong with that. But remember that reporters are trained to be skeptical of information and the people who provide it, as well they should be, unless they know and trust the source or can verify facts through numerous sources.

On one occasion while working at a national organization, we had a meeting with the editorial board (a few of the top editors and reporters) at a big daily newspaper. Even before the start of the opening pleasantries, a senior columnist on the paper looked around the room and said, "Are any of you PR agency people? If so, you can't stay." In fact, there were no agency people there (a colleague and I worked in corporate communication at our organization and we did not have anyone with us from a PR firm).

But meanwhile, in a land far away (a couple of floors below her in the newsroom) at least some of the paper's reporters surely were on the phone with PR agency, government, and corporate PR people who could provide story ideas and put them in touch quickly with good information sources. Reporters depend on PR people and other people in business at least some of the time, to help them identify good story ideas and to reach noteworthy people.

Prepackaging Stories Makes the Reporters Jobs Easier

What is pitching? Pitching is the art of proposing a good story idea to the right reporter at the right time. It's not difficult and it pays big dividends. In essence, you are doing some of the reporter's work for him or her— prepackaging a story idea, providing a few facts and maybe a good source or two—to make it easy for the reporter to visualize and write an article.

Before You Pitch A Story, You Should Do The Following:

• **Picture the completed story** and headline exactly as you would like to see it in the paper. What are the specific points you would like to see made about your organization, product, or service? Make sure to include your "must-say messages." (See the next chapter.) Write them down. Remember, if you can't picture the way a story will turn out, it is unlikely that you can convey the story idea to a reporter in your pitch.

• **Decide what kind of a story you are pitching.** If the facts are newsworthy enough, they may comprise a story unto themselves. If not, are they part of a trend? Do they support or refute something that has been a hot story in the media lately? For example, if you have an app that warns people about local traffic jams, you might want to pitch it to reporters who cover urban sprawl as well as those who cover new gadgets, cars, the workplace, time management, and consumer technology.

• **Be patient but persistent.** Unless you have breaking news, your story idea probably can wait a few days until the reporter has time to listen. It's no different than following up on a job interview or a sales call. Show some initiative but make it quick:

Sue: "Hi, this is Sue Smith from XYZ Co., I just sent you a release marked 'Better Gas Mileage in 60 Minutes' about a new piece of hardware we make that will increase a car's gas mileage by 15% and costs only $50 to install on most cars. Since you cover environmental and transportation issues, I thought you would be interested. Are you interested?"

Reporter: "Yes, but I can't talk about it now. I'm on deadline for another story."

Sue: "Can I call you back in a couple of days?"

Reporter: "Sure. That would be OK."

Sue: "Thanks. I sent you a press release with the basic information and I'll call you in a couple of days."

Now, you have:

1. Given the reporter some news and opened the door to discuss your information when the reporter is able to pay attention to it.

2. Demonstrated your professionalism by respecting the reporter's time and showed that you did your homework before you called.

Let's start with an example of ways to create easy PR wins. Here's a fun one. The Washington, D.C. region where I live is a big convention town. An international postal organization asked us to help publicize its national conference here. They especially wanted TV coverage. The problems were: 1) garden-variety conventions themselves are of little interest to press per se and 2) postal issues, frankly, are pretty bland and don't lend themselves to the visuals needed of television.

But we found a solution: two young and handsome Australian entrepreneurs were scheduled to speak at the conference and demonstrate the experimental use of delivery drones in their native country. Our "pitch" to TV assignment editors: do a story on delivery drones (a big topic in the news in general) and come interview two young guys from Australia where drone delivery is already being tested.

It worked. After interviewing the Aussies with their drones, TV crews also interviewed our client who was president of the postal association, and helped increase awareness of delivery issues and policies worldwide. We'll talk in much greater detail in later chapters about how to find colorful stories and how to interest press in covering them.

Who to Woo? Pick the Right and Reporters

Start with a good story idea and then determine which publications or broadcast outlets reach the people who can do you the most good, starting with potential customers. Then study the publications and choose reporters who have written stories that closely match the one you have in mind. Those are the reporters to contact.

• **Never pitch the same story to two reporters on the same publication** at the same time. Big no-no. If by some chance they are both interested, you will have to tell one that you have proposed it to another. One or both will be angry that you have wasted their time. Even worse, they might both start working on the story without your knowledge and look foolish to their editor. Bye-bye credibility (yours). Better to have a handful of story pitches in the works at a number of publications.

• **Which experts' names will you provide to the reporters** if they interested in your story pitch? Make sure to notify those experts ahead of time and make sure they are "on message."

• **Timing is critical to good pitching.** Understand deadlines. If you want to contact morning-newspaper reporters, columnists, and beat reporters, do so between 10 a.m.—when most of them have settled into work—and early afternoon when they start sweating their deadlines. Assignment editors at TV stations are receptive to pitch calls in the morning, as they are just starting to think about their evening newscasts. At weekly papers and magazines, call the day after the publication goes to the printer to be sure you are not calling on deadline.

• **Call reporters during "off" hours,** when few others are likely to be calling. Although news coverage is a 24-hour operation, some days are slower than others. Print, TV, and radio reporters work on Christmas Day, New Year's Day, and Thanksgiving, for example. And on Sunday morning, for that matter. Those are generally slower times with less news, and thus reporters will be more inclined to hear your pitch. But it can still be a crapshoot, depending on the day, the paper, and the editors you reach.

On "off" hours, there may be only two or three frantic people on an entire city desk trying to get out the next day's local news, for example. A bit of trial and error will tell you what you need for the outlets in which you are interested.

Be Friendly Even if You are Not Friends

A newspaper columnist I knew worked Sundays putting the finishing touches on his regular Monday column. I'd call him at his office occasionally on Sundays when I had something useful and we'd talk about work and just about anything else that was on his mind. Sometimes, I think he was just glad to hear a friendly voice on a quiet day. Our relationship developed closely enough that when my two children were born, three years apart, he made mention of it both times in his column.

Seriously? National Lasagna Day?

Recently I did some work for a national Italian restaurant chain that was opening up a new location in my region. I wanted to get the chef on a regional morning TV program so, with a bit of searching, I found out that National Lasagne Day was coming up (yes, every day in America is National "Something" Day).

I called the producer and asked her who she was having on the show for that day – no one yet, of course, since I was the one who told her about the upcoming National Lasagne Day. I told her our chef was an expert on making lasagna (seriously, is there an Italian chef who is not?) and he was booked on the show. It went very well and he was able to get in a few comments about the restaurant's recent opening.

Do Your Own Stunts

Stunts or "PR Theater" are good ways to get attention, but you need to create actual attention-getters or your pitching efforts will fall flat. The word "stunt" has a negative connotation but if done well, stunts can shine a positive media spotlight on topics that can range from serious to hilarious. To pull off a successful stunt, you need to combine your skills in coming up with story ideas (from Chapter 10) and pitching them to the right press at the right time.

You are already familiar with stunts because they have been around forever. They include activities such as:

• Blimps flying over a sporting event

• Fundraising concerts with superstar musicians

• Movie costars' romantic affairs

• Oprah Winfrey giving away cars to everyone on her show

• A man crossing the U.S. in a wheelchair to draw attention to medical research funding

• Odd competitions such as an annual street race in which waiters carry full trays of drinks as they run

• Radio show call-in contests

Try thinking in a completely different way about pitching your stories—pick story ideas and publications that your competitors will likely ignore. The added benefit is that you'll reach a potential customer base that you might have otherwise missed. This does not take the place of pitching to your typical industry press, of course, but rather, it expands your possibilities.

Man Bites Dog Stories

Here are some story ideas that are a bit out of the ordinary, any of which if published could lead to the interviewees getting calls from prospective clients:

• A chiropractor interviewed in a magazine for rock drummers
• A drama coach interviewed in a legal journal (how to be convincing to a jury)
• An interior designer in a magazine for gas-station owners (maybe something like: "Fixing up your bathroom and putting out fresh flowers will make your whole gas station seem more welcoming.")
• A dermatologist interviewed in a magazine for nudists
• A yoga instructor interviewed in a magazine for frequent airline, train, and auto travelers

AP, Reuters, Bloomberg and Dow Jones

Remember to include the wire services in your pitching. Their reach is huge. Among the wire services, the Associated Press (AP), Reuters, Bloomberg and Dow Jones are the largest. Unlike PR Newswire and the other press release distributors, wire services make their money from receivers of the news: subscriber newspapers, broadcasters, and news websites worldwide. Many of the stories you read in your newspaper and hear on TV and radio originated with reporters from these services.

The best way to pitch a story idea to AP is through its local bureaus, listed at ap.org/pages/contact/contact.html. Check online or call the bureau to find out which reporter covers the type of news you are pitching.

Reuters works a bit differently. Press releases are passed to Reuters via release distribution services such as PR Newswire, Business Wire, or Market Wire, so if you use one of those services, you're pretty well guaranteed that Reuters will see your release. Dow Jones Newswires (djnewswires.com) limits its coverage to public companies—corporate news that serves its business clients.

You can reach them through services like PR Newswire but if you have corporate news of a level that would get the attention of a paper like The Wall Street Journal (which Dow Jones publishes), you can call your local Dow Jones bureau (the directory is at djnewswires.com/us/ContactUs.htm), ask for the person who covers your type of news, and then send the person a concise press release. Dow Jones also provides news to CNBC and radio stations in the U.S., so they have a pretty big footprint.

Worksheet: Reporter Call Log
(Keeping track of the news media outreach activities)

Name	News Outlet	Date	Story Idea	Outcome
1.				
2.				
3.				
4.				
5.				
6.				
7.				
8.				

Tips for Becoming
a Hot News Source

"I worry incessantly that I might be too clear." - **Alan Greenspan, former chairman of the Federal Reserve**

Chapter Summary: You Are an Expert in Something. Flaunt It

1. Get to know reporters before you have a story to pitch. Have coffee or lunch with the top local reporters who are important to you. Then, when you do have a story to pitch, they'll already know you and your organization.

2. Make a list of stories to pitch to reporters. Start with trends in your industry that could involve your organization.

3. Consider conducting a "press tour," a series of meetings with the top reporters at your industry's publications. Combine these meetings with your regular business travel.

Want to know what the national economy is going to do in the next 12 months? Sure, who doesn't? How about a tip on what Congress or the stock market are going to do? Watch the network or cable business programs for a few minutes and— voilà!—an expert will tell you. How about prognostications in politics? Sports? Finance? Business? Sure, we got 'em too. I live in the Washington, D.C., area, a region that boasts more media-savvy experts or "pundits" per square yard than any city in the world.

Consider all of the agencies of government and the hundreds of thousands of people who toil there. Add to that the technology, biotechnology, real estate, construction, and other industries, and you get a buffet of experts from which reporters can pick as information sources. Chances are, you live in or near an area with a sizable number of experts. You may even be one of them.

The Face That Launched a Thousand Clips

Larry Sabato is one such person. He is a professor of politics at the University of Virginia. Hardly a week goes by that Sabato is not quoted by our biggest all-news radio station (even today, as I am writing this) and other media outlets on stories that deal with national and state politics. The reason? He knows his stuff and he is always available when reporters need him on deadline.

He's not a big star, not a celebrity—just a college professor and author using his hard-earned knowledge and plenty of media savvy and self-effacing humor—to gain visibility for his institution and himself.

Sabato says that, in addition to really knowing your subject matter, there are two other important requirements needed to earning your punditry wings. "First, you need to learn and practice the ability to communicate your knowledge effectively to a general audience. And then you really need to get out there.

Start by writingshort articles or commentary and sending themto reporters and others who are interested inyour subject. It takes time, but eventually theywill seek you out." Sabato says that once you arequoted in the media, publicity becomes a self-perpetuating cycle that leads to more and more coverage as you are discovered by other reporters.

Good news sources like Sabato get their press calls returned right away and receive good coverage in the media. It works this way: Someone is quoted a couple of times in a newspaper, giving him (or her) legitimacy and conferring authority upon his words. TV and radio producers see his name in print and call to interview him in their stories on the air. Appearances on TV and radio then add the luster of visibility to his opinion. Legitimacy, authority, and visibility. Even one of those attributes will qualify you as a media "expert." Having all three can get you elected to Congress.

When I was a reporter at U.S. News & World Report magazine, hardly a day went by that I didn't get a call from some young PR person calling me to say that his or her CEO was going to be in town and would I like to interview the person. My usual answer was "Why?" Did the person have a story for me, or at least some tidbit of news that I could turn into an item? Did his or her company make a product or provide a service that was directly related to what I covered?

Was it a person of note who might be a good source later— a good contact who could lead me to other good contacts? Too often, the caller did not have answers to any of those questions. Mostly, they did not know because 1) they had never read any of my stories and were unfamiliar with my beat, and 2) they did not take the time to develop a story idea for which their CEO could be a good source.

You might be an expert among people with your particular skill set, your company, your industry, your region, your competitors, and your employees. If The Wall Street Journal and CNBC are doing stories on an issue dealing with your industry, they need to talk with somebody. Why should they not quote you?

Let's discuss the ways in which you can insert yourself into the media mix and become a good source.

Don't Be A "Flack" or "Spinner"

Don't confuse being a good source with being a "flack" for your organization. A flack—an aptly derogatory term that is often used to describe all PR people—is someone who will say or do almost anything to get a story into the press. Or, they constantly pester reporters with useless information about every little activity in their organization.

The difference between being a good source and a flack is not a fine line. It's a four-lane highway that separates people who can work with the media over the long term to create win-win relationships, and others who will say or do anything to get in the paper at least once—and that's usually as far as they get. Burn a reporter even once—or keep calling her with news-free story ideas—and it will be near impossible to get back into her good graces.

No book about PR would be complete without at least mentioning the term "spin." It is a pejorative, and people who practice the technique earn a reputation for being untrustworthy. Spin is the use of deceptive, grossly selective, or manipulative information to influence opinion.

Political organizations and individuals are accused most often of "spinning" information although it can happen in any industry. In its most blatant form, spin is often used by state-run media to publish information that shows their governments only in a favorable light.

Tips for Becoming a Great News Source

- **Know who you are trying to reach among potential customers.** What do they read, listen to, and watch? Narrow the list of media outlets to those that are the most important to you and determine which reporters cover your "beat." Introduce yourself to those reporters. Make an introductory call or, if they are willing, meet with them.

- **What's Your Value?** Describe immediately why you are of value to them as a source not only for stories about your organization, but about the industries they cover in general. For example, if you have been in the widget business for 20 years, explain to the reporter that you know the industry, the main players, your competition, and upcoming developments in the technology. Also point out that you can lead them to other good sources in the industry. Trust me, once you have established your credentials, you will have the opportunity to brag about your company and its news.

- **Read everything.** You never know where story ideas will come from. When I get my car serviced, I skip the ancient issues of People magazine in the waiting room and look at publications aimed at car dealers, mechanics, and auto racing. At the dentist's office, I look at magazines for dentists and hygienists.

- **Other Worlds Out There:** You'd be amazed at the worlds that exist beyond your day-to-day planet. Maybe you have a software company that provides design solutions for manufacturing, for example. While waiting for your dental checkup, you read that the dental industry is looking for new types of disposable surgical instruments. You might be the only software engineer in the country to be aware of that for a week. You contact the "American Society of Dentists Who Are Looking for New Inventions" and set up a pitch meeting. You are the first in the door.

- **Understand information technology.** Be fluent with the Internet. (See Chapter 8.) Whether you are in your 20s or 70s, face it: You live in an internet world. Understand blogs and visit a few of them regularly. Find reliable news websites and check them every day. No matter how busy you are, you should make time to use the

Internet to stay abreast of news within your industry, your competition, and business in general. Check your competitors' websites at least once a week.

- **Create story ideas that incorporate what your organization is doing.** Pitch trends that might include not only your organization but others' as well—even if they have to be one or two of your competitors. For example, you sell telescopes and you just came out with a new model. Hardly a story, of course, unless it has been installed at the Griffith Observatory. But if you can provide statistics showing that more and more teens and millenials are getting into amateur astronomy, forming clubs, tracking space debris, beating the big guys in finding meteors, and are taking a special interest in viewing Mars as a destination for the future— that's a story.

- **Look for Experts:** Get the names of club presidents who can provide statistics, NASA officials, national sales figures, and, best of all, customers who just bought your new telescope model. Get permission to provide their names to reporters who cover science, teen trends, astronomy, business, hobbies, or new gadgets. Put together short, written story pitches and email them to the proper reporters.

- **Take new reporters under your wing.** A young reporter, one either just out of college or new to a particular beat, will certainly appreciate someone who can brief him on the industry he is covering, give him a lead on developments that will make good stories, and invite him to local industry meetings and introduce him around. Be a gateway into your industry. Over time, those reporters will see you as someone who can be counted upon for news. They will call you to be included in their stories. Plus, helping young people simply is the right thing to do.

- **Be Available:** During a crisis involving your company (see Chapter 17) be accessible to reporters. You don't need to give them information harmful to your organization, of course, just the courtesy of a return call. If you can't comment on a situation, say so. If it is a sensitive personnel matter, say so. A restrictive legal issue, say so. This can be a stressful time.

- **Cultivate Relationships:** As corporate communication director for an organization some years ago, I had a good relationship with a senior reporter whose professional style, especially on the phone, was sheer bullying. Most of the time, he demanded the facts about an issue and wanted them NOW. On those occasions when I could not give him whathe wanted, he screamed and yelled andthreatened to call my boss. I'd calmlyoffer to transfer the call to my boss, knowing he'ddecline. A week or two later, we'd laughabout it. I know he respected the fact that—even on those occasions when I could not give him all of the information he wanted—he could reach me at work or at home at any hour.

- **Beat reporters to the phone.** Reporters are going to quote someone, so it might as well be you. Keep a list of reporters you would call for breaking-news stories that can help raise your visibility. Call those reporters immediately when something newsworthy happens. Offer them a good source for the story. Maybe you sell camping and climbing equipment. You hear on the news that a teenage girl is the first of her age to reach the top of Mt. Everest. After 20 years in the business, you know that new survival equipment has helped make that sort of thing possible. Jot out some notes on climbing equipment and techniques that have been developed recently and call editors at publications that deal with adventure, sports, camping, mountain climbing, teens, and travel. Post this information on your social media platforms. Offer your credentials immediately and reporters why they should want to talk with you. You have just delivered to them an "expert" who they did not have to find themselves. Nice work.

- **Make someone on your team available to reporters** 24 hours per day, every day if you have a large enough staff. Nothing will garner your company a big kiss from reporters more than enabling them to reach a good news source at 2:00 a.m. on a Saturday if necessary.

- **Don't forget freelancers or "stringers."** Freelance writers are always hungry for good stories. They don't get a lot of perks—invitations to fancy parties or appearances on TV and radio—so they will appreciate attention at least as much as regular reporters. The best way to find freelancers is to take note of their bylines in the publications, blogs and other things you read and also ask editors for some names and contact information. Get to know them and their primary interests. They can be valuable allies in pitching a story. Your great story ideas help put money in their pockets, and the publicity helps put money in yours.

- **Call reporters with tips that will lead to stories,** but make sure the information is of value. If you heard at a public meeting that the top three companies in your industry are advocating a new design standard for super widgets, that's news! Even if your company is not one of the three, the reporter will realize quickly that you are a good news source and not just a flack for your company. Give the reporter contact names to flesh out the story. In the example above, you may get quoted reacting to the news in the story.

Hit the Road or Phone Jack: Conduct a Press Tour to Meet with Your Most Important Media

A "press tour" is exactly what it sounds like: a series of visits to meet with editors and reporters at the media outlets that reach your audiences. Your press tour may be local or spread out across the world. The point of a press tour is two-fold. First, you want to establish face-to-face relationships with reporters and editors so you can get their attention when you have news; the second is to convince them why they should care about your company, your products or your services in their news coverage. The "why" is critical.

Try a mini press tour to see if it is a good tactic for you. Set up a series of meetings with publications and broadcasters in your immediate region. You'll see quickly how best to conduct these get-togethers. Then, if you like the results, take it on the road. These press meetings—sometimes called "editorial board meetings"—can be scheduled in conjunction with other business travel: meetings, trade shows, etc.

Make a list of the important publications in your industry and cross-reference the list with executive travel schedules. For example, if you are in the online-education business, contact IT and education editors in cities you will be visiting and provide a good story pitch as incentive for them to meet with you.

The best way to set up an editorial board meeting is through a reporter that you may already know. Ask him or her to pitch the idea to colleagues and organize the meeting. A single PR person is enough to keep everyone on schedule and handle details. Don't bring a giant posse of "handlers" and don't outnumber the media. Everyone in your group should have something to add to the conversation. Otherwise, leave them in the lobby reading the back issues of TIME.

Don't overstay your welcome. Editors and reporters are frantically busy people. If there is an hour set aside for the meeting, make it 45 minutes.

A good 45-minute press-tour meeting should go something like this:

• Introductions and small talk. (about 3 minutes)

• The primary person on your team should start the conversation. Thank the editors for the invitation. Tell them exactly why you are there: 1) The readers of this newspaper are important to us because 2) we have a product or service that will be of strong interest to them, 3) we want to establish a face-to-face relationship with the appropriate editors and reporters here, and 4) we can be excellent sources for trend stories in our industry. (5 minutes)

• Tell the editors how your product, service, or cause will be of strong interest to their audience. Give them any timely news about a new product or service. (10 minutes)

• Give them time to ask questions. (15 minutes)

• Ask the editors which part of what you have told them was most interesting and find out if they are working on any stories for which you can provide good sources. (10 minutes)

• Wrap up and goodbye. (2 minutes)

The most senior attendee should follow up with a handwritten note to the top editor. When you have some hot news, call the appropriate editor, remind him/her that you met at the editorial board meeting and then pitch the news in the form of a good story idea. A good press tour should include TV and radio stations when possible.

Pitch assignment editors at local stations with your news before you leave home and try to schedule on-air interviews. Although a press tour can be time-consuming, if you target the right news outlets, it is time well spent.

The Satellite Media Tour

You can get excellent broadcast press exposure without traveling out of town by conducting what is called a satellite media tour. A satellite media tour (SMT) is a series of back-to-back television or radio interviews that allows a spokesperson to be interviewed – sitting in a local studio -- by multiple television stations and radio stations and networks within a few hours. The logistics are relatively simple but if you've not done this yourself before, it's probably good to hire some help.

Here's how it works: TV and radio stations around the country are asked in advance if they'd be interested in interviewing an expert on a particular topic. The expert sits in front of a camera in a studio listening to questions with an earpiece. The audio/video parts of the interview are uploaded to stations on a satellite channel. SMTs generally take about four hours of a spokesperson's time, and typically take place from 6:00 to 10:00 a.m. Eastern.

Interviews are typically scheduled in five-minute windows allowing for breaks in the schedule for interviewees to get up, walk around, and touch up their makeup.

Stations and networks then can download video/sound bites and b-roll via a satellite feed, stream, video download or request a hard copy. A broadcast e-mail is sent to alert stations and networks of the soundbites and availability of the video footage. (B-roll is a term that refers to pre-prepared video footage reporters and producers can use for coverage of your story in addition to anything they may shoot themselves).

Think Visually

Susan Matthews Apgood, president of News Generation, Inc., says, "The biggest advantage of an SMT is saving on travel time and money. A tour allows spokespeople to 'visit' 15 to 20 media outlets in just one morning. And, with the technology of satellites and high definition, the quality is just as good as being on site for the interviews. Clients hire us because of our relationships. We are constantly booking media tours for both radio and television."

She adds, "With television interviews, you want to show the story as visually as possible. So, not only do you see the spokesperson during the interview, b-roll is also included in each interview. This allows the opportunity to visually tell the story as well."

An SMT is not cheap, but it is certainly less expensive than hitting the road with hotel rooms, airfare, food, etc. News Generation, Inc, for example, charges about $29,000 for a national satellite media tour. That includes completing 15 to 18 interviews in one morning. For a radio media tour, the budget for 15 interviews, which is average for national outreach, is $7,300. A tour that is geographically targeted to certain states or markets -- a combination of both radio and television interviews -- is roughly $25,000.

13

Turn Your Whole
Team Into "Champions"

"Someone is sitting in the shade today because someone planted a tree a long time ago." —**investor Warren Buffett**

Chapter Summary: Well, No One Ever Asked Us!

1. The reason your organization may not have a group of people who are your "cheerleaders" is that you've probably never asked them. So, go ahead and ask!

2. Almost everyone you know can be an advocate for your organization: customers, board members, employees, vendors, family, and friends. Ask them to mention you whenever they can in formal communication such as press interviews and presentations as well as on informal occasions such as networking.

3. Treat your champions like royalty. Include them in your company news and events.

The CEO of a midsize company once told me he was shy about asking customers and others to "champion" his organization—that is, to provide testimonials, speak to the press, and talk with potential customers. He was self-conscious about asking for help. "My customers are busy with their own businesses and don't have time for this," he said.

Then one morning, after meeting with a client who was a prominent member of the industry in which they both worked, he asked the client if he'd be willing to speak with prospects if the occasion arose. To his surprise, the customer said he'd be glad to. In fact, the client went even further. He was happy with the service he was getting and, as a result, said he already sang the company's praises whenever he could. "Now, give me the names of your top half-dozen prospects, the ones who are on the fence, and I will call and tell them why they should hire you."

The CEO was floored and gave him the names. Within a few weeks, he had landed a couple of the prospects. The deciding factor for them was a glowing and unsolicited personal testimonial from the customer they knew and respected. His strong endorsement, backed by the fact that he was a loyal customer himself, made all of the difference.

Your company has customers, members, vendors, board members, and others who are rooting for you to succeed. You just have to ask! Wouldn't you root for and help out an organization that you liked and that provided you with good service? I call them "champions."

I Could Buy Cake, Fix My Car *Anywhere*, but I Don't

A bakery just opened up not far from my house and it looks great; the food is of excellent quality and the people are warm and obviously glad to get my business. So I give it to them—I'd rather destroy my diet with them than with anyone else. I am one of this bakery's champions. The same goes for my local auto-repair shop.

They have been fair, skilled, andfriendly for years. They value me as a customer. They are not always the cheapestaround, but that's where I go, and I have told anumber of friends about them. If they askedme to call a customer or two, I'd do it becauseI am one of this garage's champions.

I have anindependent movie theatre near my house thatI like because the owner comes out right afterthe previews and asks the whole audience, "Sowhich of these movies would you come watchif I ordered them?" He then gives out free popcorn and sodas to people unfortunate enoughto have to sit in the front row when the theatreis sold out. How can you not love that? Myfamily, friends, and I have told scores of people about this place. I am one of that movie theater's champions.

Champions may not necessarily have a vested interest in your success except that they are happy with the service you provide, they like you and your team personally, they admire your drive, they want to help you push ahead of the competition, and they would be proud to look back one day and know that they helped an industry powerhouse when it was just a few people in a little rented office.

Champions Can Include Just About Anyone You Know:

- Customers
- Former customers
- Board members
- Members of your trade association or chamber of commerce
- Employees
- Former employees
- Vendors
- Partners
- Investors
- Friends
- Family members
- Neighbors

Six Benefits That Champions Can Provide:

1. They can speak with reporters when necessary.

2. They can write testimonials for your website and your marketing and sales kits. (You can draft these testimonials yourself and have them modify the words according to their own style; there's nothing wrong with that.) Make sure your collection of testimonials addresses the language in those all-important corporate messages we learned about in Chapter 4.

3. You can write an article for their byline in an industry publication.

4. Champions can call prospects and brag about how happy they are with your products and services.

5. They can serve as members of an advisory committee.

6. They can mention your company in presentations they make to industry groups.

Six Ways to Treat Your Champions Like the Royalty They Are:

1. Keep them up to date on your organization. Make them feel like part of the "family." Send champions your company newsletters, press releases, press clips, and other public communication.

2. Invite them to an all-staff meeting once a year to get to know your team. If they are customers, have them tell your employees firsthand how your company's work really makes a difference.

3. Cross-promote their organizations with your own. If you have a newsletter, mention them occasionally as a company you like. Put information about them on your website.

4. Send reporters their way if they would make good sources for stories, even if the stories have nothing to do with your company.

5. Send them a small token of appreciation once in a while.

6. Invite them to industry events as your guest.

Don't Forget One Of Your Most Important Groups of Champions

Internal PR: Employees make up one of your most important publics. Staffers who are treated well and enjoy their work are happy to talk about it with others. Unfortunately, even in midsize companies, employees are often overlooked in the communication chain, learning about company developments by reading about them in the newspaper or hearing about them on the company grapevine. This can be destructive to morale, productivity, cooperation, and trust. CEOs love to say in speeches that their most important resources are their employees. If that is indeed true in your organization, show them.

Public relations and human resources departments should work together to ensure that employees understand that they are valued. From an internal-PR standpoint, treat your employees at least as well as any of your other audiences. Here are five rules to remember when communicating with employees.

1. Meet them face to face. The first, and easiest rule, is what former General Electric CEO Jack Welch, one of the world's most respected business leaders, called "management by walking around." Literally, it means that senior executives should get out of their offices and meet with employees in every part of the company.

For our purposes, we'll call it "Internal PR by walking around." It accomplishes two important things. First, it shows employees that you care enough about what they do to come downstairs and see for yourself. Second, you can learn a lot just by asking people. Find out what they do. Ask them about the family photos on their desks, where they live, what they like about the job, and what bugs them. Most important, ask (not necessarily in front of their supervisors) for suggestions on making the company better, making products or services better, and making their working lives better.

Don't just visit managers; visit every level of the company. If you are sincere and come across as a person who is comfortable doing this, they will open up to you. The very worst thing you can do meet with employees and spend the whole time talking about yourself – showing complete disinterest in your employees. If you're that person, stay in your office.

2. Most companies have email newsletters. Include company news about important as well as mundane things—anything from details about a new product to an update on the new phone system. Include links to newspaper stories about the company, your competition, and other industry news. Include fairly innocent personal stuff about employees (with their permission). This might include a wedding photo, a travel photo, a son or daughter's college graduation or achievement in athletics, the arts, or other avocation. If an employee just ran the Boston Marathon, for example, include a photo of the person crossing the finish line.

3. Don't adopt the old Pravda model. When times are bad in the company, explain why. Don't gloss over it by running wedding photos in the newsletter when the company is getting ready to file Chapter 11. Be mindful, though, that anything in the company newsletter could be made public.

4. Create a well-designed and useful password-protected Intranet site. But, again, don't assume that anything posted on the site will remain within the company. Don't print anything in your company newsletter or on the Intranet that you would be distraught seeing on the front page of your local newspaper. In addition to the kinds of things listed above in the company newsletter, post all of the company's external communication—marketing materials, messages, speeches, etc.—in pdf. format for easy access and download. Always send news releases to staff at the same time they go out to press.

5. Encourage managers to have impromptu lunches with their staff members once a month, providing food and an informal atmosphere. They should spend part of the time socializing and the rest talking shop. If the manager engenders trust and comfort in his or her employees, people will open up and offer good suggestions.

Management and PR by Walking Around in the Panamanian Jungle

Now this is internal PR by walking around. During my stint in the Army, while stationed in Panama, I was assigned for about a week to cover a joint training exercise between a few hundred U.S. and Panamanian forces in the middle of the jungle. Early one morning, as a thick mist rose from the jungle floor, we found a large clearing and decided to take a break.

Morale was poor, given that the troops were exhausted from the heat, humidity, mosquitoes, and the training itself. After a few minutes, we could hear a helicopter in the distance. As the thwack-thwack-thwacking grew louder, we realized that the aircraft intended to land inside our clearing. Sure enough, a big green helicopter with Panamanian military markings set down gently into the space.

Before the blades even stopped, out jumped Omar Torrijos, commander of the Panamanian National Guard, "Maximum Leader of the Panamanian Revolution" and "Supreme Chief of the Government" (and predecessor to the even-more infamous dictator Manuel Noriega).

Torrijos was dressed right out of Hollywood central casting: tall, olive-drab fatigues, shiny black jackboots, cowboy hat with the sides turned up, two holstered, Patton-like, pearl-handled .45 pistols, and a giant cigar. We stood stunned at the sight; it was like an apparition from a dream.

Most of the American GIs had no idea who this guy was. But the young Panamanian troops recognized him immediately and were thunderstruck at seeing their commander-in-chief standing right in front of them. Torrijos shook hands for 15 minutes, wished his boys and ours well, and then was gone, up through the mist and into the sky. Just like that.

Immediately, the morale of the Panamanian troops picked up. They were smiling, slapping each other on the back, and working with renewed energy. The visit by their "Maximum Leader" had underscored for them the importance of what they were doing. The good morale was contagious and it even spread to the American boys who, having met their first genuine Central American dictator, now had something interesting to write home about.

How to Shine When Doing Press Interviews

"The secret of success is sincerity. Once you can fake that, you've got it made." **-- Jean Giraudoux**

Chapter Summary: Learn to Take "Yes" for an Answer

1. Find the reporter's last couple of published stories. Understand his/her style.
2. Ask the reporter, "What do you plan to ask me?" Sometimes they will tell you.
3. If the interview is in your office, remove distractions.
4. "Bridge" back into your messages when appropriate.
5. Speak "through" the reporter directly to your audience.
6. Speak in clear, short sound bites.
7. Take "yes" for an answer. Make your point; stop talking.
8. Don't "break into jail" by providing drifting into tangential topics.

Three Out of Four Ain't Bad

Getting your story into the news media is the most sought-after method for raising visibility. There are four levels of media exposure. This book is designed to help you achieve significant success in the first three. They are:

1. Comfort with occasional interviews and getting mentioned in the media

2. Increasing your visibility—and your company's—in the industry through frequent traditional media exposure and using social media tools

3. Actively seeking high visibility in the media and becoming a "pundit." You can do this by:

> a. Having good information on a subject and an ability to explain it well
> b. Being "on message"
> c. Developing personal relationships with reporters who cover your industry
> d. Becoming a "name" in your industry, your locale, or both
> e. Having the chutzpah to comment on just about any subject in which you have expertise
> f. Being available 24/7 to talk with reporters (The ability to do an interview with The New York Times by cell phone while waiting in line for a ride with your kids at Disney World qualifies, although I don't recommend it.)

4. Get your own show and interview major Hollywood stars who confess that, as teenagers, they were gawky, unpopular kids with braces who could never get a date. Sorry—that's a different book.

Keep an Eye on the Little Red Light!

When I worked for PBS one of our senior executives, who'd had little exposure to the media, was being interviewed by the Washington bureau of a TV network about a controversial issue regarding children's programming. I won't name the network (ABC).

The taping was to take place one evening in the executive's home—rarely a good place for an interview (too many distractions including family, dog, phones, neighbors, repairmen, etc.)—but necessary due to his busy schedule. The day before the interview, "Jack" and I reviewed his top message points and potential questions pertaining to the issue. He was ready.

The interviewer, a woman in her 30s, and her cameraman showed up at the appointed time. After a few niceties, she launched straight into the issue at hand—criticism PBS had received about a particular program we were offered but did not air. Jack, well practiced over the previous few days, handled the core question well.

He was informative and right on message. Apparently, though, he did not give the answer the woman came for. Undaunted, she then asked the same question again, but worded it a bit differently. Again, Jack repeated the answer verbatim. Again came the question again. Same answer. Same question. Same answer. The exchange took place two or three more times with the same result. Finally, sensing she was not going to get the sound bite she came for, the interviewer stood up and thanked Jack for his time.

Jack then relaxed and loosened his tie. As the woman was putting her notebook back in her purse and fumbling with her car keys, the cameraman who, up to this point, had not said a word, spoke up. Joking with Jack, the cameraman said, "OK, now you can tell us what you really think."

Jack, unaware that the camera was still rolling, was about to shoot back a clever wisecrack. Cutting him off mid smirk, I pointed out to Jack that he was still being interviewed on camera. "See that little red light?" I said. That ended the evening with what could have been a very embarrassing moment on network television.

"We Start Bombing in Five Minutes." Is the Mic On?

The lesson here is that if you can see a camera or a microphone, or have reason to believe that there is one nearby, assume that it is on, pointed at you and that you will be on the record for anything you say, no matter how much you protest later. Even presidents—with their armies of hyper-vigilant communication people—can learn this the hard way.

You may know of President Reagan's comment near what he thought was an unplugged microphone: "My fellow Americans, I am pleased to tell you I just signed legislation which outlaws Russia forever. The bombing will begin in five minutes." The mic was on and his comment aired that night on TV and radio and in the next day's newspapers.

White House communication staff had to deal with that comment and the press fallout for days afterward. One might also assume there to have been a spate of underwear changing in the Kremlin. And now, with smartphones everywhere – they are essentially TV cameras – there is no such thing as privacy in any public or semi-public place. Just ask Mitt Romney, whose comment about the "47%" helped to sink his presidential campaign.

Treat every interview like a game you plan to win. Come in with a strategy, take it seriously, and don't let up until the final buzzer sounds. That's it for the basketball metaphors, I promise. But decide *why* you are doing the interview. Generally, the reason you should want to do an interview is to *make a good case to change or strengthen your audience's thinking and/or behavior to your viewpoint.*

Talking *Through* the Reporter Will Help You Reach Your Audience More Effectively

Now that you know how to create and use your main messages, here is another important concept to remember in any interview: Talk *through* the reporter directly to the audience. Yes, through. Why? Because an interview is not a conversation in the usual sense. You are instead engaging the reporter as a medium (thus, the term "media") to reach your intended audience.

Here's how you do it: Picture a single individual you want to influence—a potential customer, for example—look into the camera or into the eyes of the interviewer and speak directly to that customer. You'll be amazed how effective that can be.

There is a temptation to treat a reporter just like any conversation partner. You've spent the first minute or two of your meeting/interview making small talk about the weather, the traffic, and your weekend. You both went to the same college. You are both golfers. Your ancestors came from the same country. You get comfortable. At this point, it may feel a bit wooden to stick to your sound bites and messages, but none of this chummy stuff is likely to end up in the interview.

Remember the PBS executive? Every time he got the same question, he gave the same answer—over and over. And guess what? His answer appeared only once in the story, exactly the way he wanted it. Remember that in an interview, most of the time what appears are only your quotes, not the reporter's questions. On television, usually all that appears of you are your sound bites.

Take the Test. What is Your "Quotability Quotient" and How Can You Raise Your Score?

Doing well in an interview just takes practice and anyone can do it. But there have been people who have a natural ability to charm the press: John F. Kennedy, Harry Truman, former Texas Governor Ann Richards, and Winston Churchill, just to name a few. What gave them that ability was equal parts charm, intelligence, grit, articulation, a touch of hubris, and a good grasp on what I call "Quotability Quotient."

What is a Quotability Quotient? I 'll be frank with you...this far into the book, I had to come up with something my publisher would think was "A Big Concept" and would cause every reader to run through the bookstore, eyes wide, waving the book, and chanting "Buy, buy, buy!" Also, it is always good for an author—especially one who majored in the humanities — to claim that he can take something that may be unquantifiable and (after many years of exacting social research, trial and error and loud lab explosions) assign it a numeric score.

So there you go. If you are standing in the bookstore aisle and happen to have flipped the book open to this page, please shout out, "My Quotability Quotient is 50!" at least once so we can move on. We'll get to the arithmetic later.

Quotability Quotient is a simple way to measure the combination of factors that will enable you to conduct a winning interview with the press. You need not be a JFK to do it. You just need to become comfortable with the idea of an interview as a business transaction (see Chapter 14) and be able to address the factors that matter most. You need to get your messages effectively into print and give the reporter his newsworthy story. (OK, her newsworthy story—don't send me emails!)

Here are a few rules to remember in creating and raising your Quotability Quotient:

• Thou shalt not be boring. Keep answers brief and easily understood. Even if you have answered a question 100 times, keep it fresh in your own mind by changing the wording somewhat while keeping the meaning. How does Adele plays "Hello" with enthusiasm at every concert? How have the cast members of "Hamilton" and "Book of Mormon" performed the shows night after night after night (and twice on Sunday) on Broadway for so long?

If you are boring, the reporter will go into a deep sleep from which he or she may never awaken, your interview will die on the vine, and your wisdom will never appear in print. Keep answers short, memorable, quotable, and newsworthy. Have mercy on the poor ink-stained wretch, especially those writing for some online news outlets where 500 words is considered thorough.

• Avoid jargon and acronyms. Using industry jargon with someone who is not in your industry is boorish, kind of like meeting a girl's parents for the first time and having them spend the whole evening telling stories about how great her old boyfriend was. Not that it ever happened to me and even if it did, I certainly would not still be ticked enough about it to mention it in a book decades later, especially in a book that has nothing to do with relationships I may or may not have had.

But I digress. Anyway, some people cling to jargon because it keeps them from having to work hard enough to really communicate with their intended audience. If Stephen Hawking can make us understand something as complex as time, space and the origins of the universe, we should be able to explain the benefits of our products, services, and organizations.

Never Assume Anything! Explain in Plain English

• Never assume a reporter understands your industry. On occasion, a newspaper or broadcast outlet will assign a reporter who is either inexperienced in general or covers a beat that is completely foreign to your industry or issue. When the person who usually covers personal finance is subbing for the person who covers, say, state politics, it could be a dangerous situation for you and your company. Recognize it early. Ask the reporter about his expertise without embarrassing him.

Offer to provide a good, solid backgrounder on your industry— maybe an hour on the phone or in person, before you even get into the news. Provide plenty of written materials including an industry backgrounder that covers the core issues, a recent story from another publication, a list of bullet points in plain English that lays out the issues at hand for the story, and provide, of course, your office, home, and cell phone number with an offer to have him call you. Then, offer to read the story before it goes into print.

Ninety-nine percent of newspapers don't permit pre-publication review, but it never hurts to ask. One thing you can do is ask the reporter, once the story is written, if he will review some of the high points with you. It is in a reporter's interest to get the story right. Make it easy for him to nail the story without making him look foolish or uninformed to his editor.

• Let your personality shine through. Put yourself in the reporter's place. We're all human and we all react the same way to other people who are colorful, energetic, and unique. If you can bring at least a bit of all of these qualities to the interview, you will have a much greater chance of getting into the story and being quoted on a regular basis.

And the Final QQ Score Is:

OK, here is the part where we quantify your ability to conduct an interview successfully. Actually, this system does work, although we're not yet ready to call Scientific American magazine. To determine your Quotability Quotient for a particular interview, rate yourself 1 to 10 on each of these five items (with 10 being the highest) and then get a total.

1. You have new and timely information to provide to the reporter (and to your key audiences).

2. You can deliver the information in taut, colorful sound bites that can stand on their own.

3. You have the self-confidence to deliver the information in an authoritative manner.

4. You are familiar with the reporter's previous work and can tailor your answers to fit the audience.

5. You have a personality—or you can at least fake one until the interview is over.

Your average score:

• **45-50:** Oprah, thanks for buying my book.

• **35-44:** You are ready to give an effective interview. Study your message points one more time and go for it.

• **20-34:** Go back to the five criteria and at least take care of numbers 1 and 2. Don't give the interview until you are ready.

• **Less than 20:** Keep practicing.

Notice how people with high visibility—actors, music stars, politicians, business moguls, etc.—nearly always use well-practiced and TV-ready sound bites. Celebrity + Quotability = Media Coverage. It's as sure a force of nature as gravity itself.

Humans Have a Gag Reflex for a Reason

Our family dog, a big black Lab mutt of some sort, is lovable but not brainy. I know this because if I take a nap on the couch, he checks on me about every 15 minutes to make sure I am not dead. He does this by putting his icy-wet nose into my open mouth, causing me to bolt up instantly, gagging and coughing. Satisfied that his master is safe, he goes back to doing whatever it is he does all day. My death would be a tragedy because, between the two of us, I'm the only one tall enough to reach the dog biscuits in the kitchen cabinet.

I bring this up only because this gag response is the same reaction I have when one of my clients is blindsided by a reporter's question. Once in a while it happens, but there is no reason to be unprepared. Make sure you have solid information and the skill to deliver the right messages effectively.

Have you ever watched an airline pilot prepare for takeoff? Even pilots with thousands of hours in the cockpit use checklists to make sure they remember every setting, switch, and dial that will ensure a safe takeoff, flight, and landing. Even if you consider yourself a veteran with the press, you should do the same. Here are the important steps to get yourself ready for an interview and ace it in the process.

The Interview "Preflight" Checklist

1. Always understand the topic completely before agreeing to an interview. Ask the reporter specifically what the questions will be about.

2. Never do an interview cold. Prepare yourself. Even if a reporter is on tight deadline, it does not necessarily mean that you are. If you get a cold call for an interview, tell the reporter you will call him back. Prepare yourself and then do your best to call back before deadline.

3. Get the information you need before an interview:

> • What is the topic? Can you find out what some of the questions might be?
> • When is the interview? What is the format?
> • How long will it take?
> • Who will do the interview and what has the person written recently on the topic?
> • Who else will be interviewed for the story?
> • If on TV or radio, will it air live or will it be recorded and edited?

4. Be cautious with reporters you don't know. Do an online search to read 2-3 of their latest stories. You want to be confident they will quote you correctly and that they will do their homework before the interview.

5. Don't duck an interview. Just because you won't talk to the reporter doesn't mean he won't write the story, and it's likely that one of your competitors, your employees, a disgruntled customer, or your ex-spouse will be glad to do an anonymous interview.

6. Learn what you can about the publication, audience, interviewer, and story. Is it going to be a general story about ethics in business, for example, or does the reporter want to talk with you specifically about your chairman's use of the company Gulfstream jet to transport his cat to a vacation home in Aspen?

7. Review the five to six "must-say" message points that make your case.

8. Visualize the "headline." What would you like the story to say? Make your messages "write" this headline and story. "Write" the headline first and work back from there. You can manage the news even if you can't control it.

9. Write out the 25 most likely questions. Pick the 10 you really don't want to have to answer and practice them until you have the answers down perfectly. Practice answers to all potential questions.

10. Arrive on time. Give yourself a few minutes to relax, think, and practice your talking points.

During an Interview, Take Command of the Situation but Be Personable

• **If it is a phone interview, clear your desk and remove distractions.** Get into the proper mindset.

• **Keep message points in front of you.** Repeat your messages two or three times during the interview to make sure they get into the story.

• **Speak *through* the reporter** to your audience. (See above.)

• **Learn to take yes for an answer.** Skilled salespeople say that once you make the sale, don't keep selling! Same goes for interviews. Once you make your point and you are sure the reporter gets it, shut up and move on. Avoid the temptation to embellish your answer for a few more minutes because you know so much about the topic at hand. (See "Don't Break Into Jail," below.)

• **Be engaging and friendly.**

• **Speak slowly.** Remember, the reporter has to understand you well enough to explain it to others.

• **Don't repeat a negative question as part of your answer;** it will end up as part of your quotes in the story. Stay positive.

• **Don't criticize your competitors by name**—you're giving them free PR. If you hammer home what makes your product or service unique, your potential customers will figure out the differences for themselves.

• **Never lie.** Just say you can't discuss a particular topic.

• **Don't guess.** "I don't know. I'll get back to you on it," is a fine answer. Say you will call back and then DO it.

• **Make your points easily understood**, e.g., use clarifying statements to get a reporter's attention to make sure he/she is focused when you give your messages:

>   • "The three critical issues are"
>   • "There are three main points to remember here"
>   • "The most important aspect of this whole situation is"
>   • "The people who will be affected by this are"
>   • "Let me summarize."

• **Let the reporter use an audio recorder for accuracy.** You can use one too for verification.

• **Do not say the reporter's name during a broadcast interview.** The person presenting the story on the air may be different from the one who interviewed you.

• **Politeness aside, avoid the temptation to use "sir" or "ma'am"** in a broadcast interview. It makes you appear subservient to the reporter. Military personnel should pay particular attention to this.

• **In a confrontational interview, stick to the high road.** Don't be defensive. Avoid emotion.

• **Always stay in control of an interview.** Even if the reporter is rapid-firing questions at you, it is OK to think before you speak. They can't quote you on something you didn't say. In this day of one-minute TV or online stories that are considered in-depth, pausing to think before answering a difficult question can be perceived as being stymied. Still, go for substance over style.

• **Never say flatly, "No comment."** It makes it appear as though you are hiding something negative. Always give a reason, even if it is noncommittal, e.g., "We can't discuss anything in litigation," "We don't discuss personnel matters," "We don't respond to rumors," or "Once our new product is ready to announce, we will do so."

• **Photography:** In most cases, print photographers travel separately from reporters. If you want to look your best in a photo, and have a choice, have photos taken in the late morning. Too early in the day, and your face may still be puffy from the pillow; too late in the afternoon, and your eyes will begin to sag from the stress of the day.

Also, control the context. You may have an actual wooden horse from a merry-go-round in your office, but do you want your picture taken on it as the photographer suggests? Be careful; look at your surroundings and what will be in the photo. You might have some souvenir bourbon bottles or a bust of Elvis on a shelf in your office. Move them out of the picture. At a social gathering, put your wine glass behind your back before you pose for a photo.

Don't Break Into Jail

No one knew about the Nixon oval office tapes until White House aide Alexander Butterfield mentioned them in an FBI interview. No one had asked him about them until long into the Watergate investigation. Ka-boom! Talk about consequences! Certainly, as a country, we were better off knowing about the tapes—all 3,700 hours of them. But the example shows how powerful the unasked question can be when it is finally asked - and answered.

Offering up damaging information you are not asked about is the same as breaking into jail. If you agree to an interview, tell the truth, but stay in control of your answers. Stick to the questions at hand and stick to your messages.

Following are a few pointers to avoid breaking to jail:

• **Don't answer questions you are not asked.**

• **Don't bait the reporter** or show off how much you know by offering up tidbits of information that will lead to difficult questions. For example, unless asked, don't say that you know something that you can't divulge.

• **Say what you want to say and then shut up.** Next question, please.

• **Don't bring up tangential topics.** They will lead you into territory for which you are unprepared.

• **Don't get personal.** For example, if the story is about your industry, don't go off on a tangent about how it relates to the business started by your old high school buddy.

• **Stay cool.** Never, ever, let your emotions show.

Whatever the Questions, You'll Shine by "Bridging" to Your Messages

Bridging is an interview technique that, when used properly, answers the question but keeps you in control of the answer. Anyone can do it with a bit of practice. What you are bridging to are your main messages so, regardless of the questions, you want your answers to include the messages. Let's say, for example, there is an industry rumor that your company is being sold. However, you are doing an interview to discuss a series of new products that you are putting on the market and are not yet in a position to discuss a sale of the company. You have your message points about the products ready to go and you have practiced possible answers to all questions including those about selling the company. Here is an effective way to bridge to your messages:

Reporter: "There is talk in the industry that you are in negotiations with your largest competitor about selling your company."

You: "Because of our success, our company is and has always been attractive to suitors, but we never discuss that sort of thing. Right now, we're just working on making our company and products the best they can be. We have a new line of wireless widgets that are already making a big splash among consumers—three new models that hospitals, police departments, and airports are excited about. They will be available for general consumer use in three months."

Reporter: "Let's just say IF you sell your company, will there be layoffs?"

You: "I can't get into hypotheticals with you, but we are known as a great place to work and we take care of our team. That's one of the reasons we are a leader in the industry and our turnover rate is less than 12%. In fact, last year, we were voted among the top five companies for women."

As you can see, the interviewee is in complete control of the interview. She/he has answered the core question (without a curt "No comment.") in a friendly and cooperative way while using the opportunity to brag about new products and the employee-friendliness of the company.

Tough Love: Media Training Means Never Having to Say You're Sorry

Even if you have been interviewed on a number of occasions and have done well, media training is important. Media training is a technique that arms you with methods you may not have used before to get your messages across. I have spent a good part of my career training CEOs and other executives to handle media interviews and can attest that even the most media savvy executive can benefit from a few pointers.

Public relations firms and companies that specialize in media training can do an excellent job in getting your executives ready to meet the press. In addition to their experience in the field, they can also ask your executives extremely difficult questions that staff members may be uncomfortable asking.

If you can afford it, check to see what they offer. Expect to pay anywhere from a few hundred dollars to thousands for a half-day or full-day training session. The price will depend on the firm you hire, how many executives need to be trained, and whether the training will include on-camera drills for improving TV-interview skills.

If, on the other hand, you want to do this frugally—especially if your available budget is near zero—recruit people on your staff with media experience, or just pick staffers who are outgoing and have a good understanding of your company to be the interrogators. Very important: Nix anyone who is afraid of your executives. They won't ask any questions worth sparring against.

Here are some tips that can save you thousands of dollars, especially if you can't afford to bring in professionals to do the training.

> • Determine who in your organization is going to speak to the media. Designate an alternate in case the other person is not available. Train only those people for now. Train others on an as-needed basis.

> • Give the trainers and the trainees your company messages ahead of time and make sure they are fluent in using them before you do any training.

> • Prepare a list of questions ahead of time and do not show them to the people being trained. Ask the hardest questions you can imagine a reporter asking. Once, we were training the CEO of a large energy company to do TV interviews. In the middle of questions about profits and a new service, we said to him out of the blue: "We heard that you've used company funds to fix up your beach house and buy a sailboat." And then someone knocked over a chair as a further distraction. The allegation wasn't true, but we wanted to get a reaction. He was speechless and stone-faced, an expression that, once he saw it on camera, he vowed never to repeat. Once he got used to our asking these types of "ambush" questions, he handled them

well.

• Record all questions and answers. Audio recordings are good; video is even better because interviewees can see body language and mannerisms. Play recordings back frequently during the training. Interviewees should see a steady improvement in their ability to use messages and answer questions confidently.

Benchmarks for successful media training should include:

• Hit all messages more than once during the interview

• Interviewee came across as confident and well informed

• Interviewee was in control of the interview and did not become defensive

Worksheet: Pre-Interview Quick Checklist

- **What is the story about?**

- **Who is our expert who will be interviewed?**

- **Who is the reporter? What other stories has he/she written?**

- **What are the 5-6 messages do we need to get into the story?**

- **What headline would we like to see on this story?**

- **What are the likely questions the interviewer will ask?**

- **How long will the interview be?**

- **Get rid of all distractions so I can focus on the interview (at least turn off cellphone).**

- **When will the article run?**

Master the TV Interview

"It's better to look good than to feel good." **-- comedian Billy Crystal**

Chapter Summary: You Look Mah-velous!

1. See the interview Checklist in Chapter 14 for general interview guidelines.
2. Television interviews generally are as much about style as substance.
3. Repeat your main messages two or three times naturally as part of the conversation so the interviewer can choose the best version of sound bites.
4. Talk directly to the interviewer. The camera and microphone will find you.
5. Gesture with your hands where appropriate.
6. Men: Don't refuse light makeup.
7. Women: Avoid large, shiny, dangling, or otherwise distracting jewelry.

Check this out on YouTube. It's old but has rarely been bested. Comedian Bob Newhart — in his sitcom ages ago—did what I consider to be the best routine ever about a hapless guy being interviewed on TV for the first time. Before the interview, the female host assures him that he'll get softball questions about how he helps people as a psychiatrist. They joke around and make small talk before the show.

But once the cameras are on, everything goes to hell. The interviewer fires off one blistering question after another, leaving Newhart confused, defensive, blushing, and, finally, speechless. (She asks him, for example, whether his psychiatric services are overpriced. He answers, "Well, we validate parking.") It's hilarious when Newhart does it. Not so funny if it happens to you.

More than 90% of communication is nonverbal, so the way you carry yourself, the way you dress, your gestures, and your facial expressions are critically important. Unless you are a bank loan officer or a DMV clerk, the human face is capable of about 10,000 distinct expressions.

Television interviews are, by far, the trickiest of all press encounters but they can also be the most rewarding. Welcome the opportunity to appear on TV, and be prepared. By remembering a few rules and practicing, anyone can look and sound big on the little screen. Generally there are three types of television interviews.

Master the TV Interview: Have Something to Say and Look Great Doing It

- **Recorded:** Your interview will be aired in its entirety or will be cut up into smaller sound bites for part of a larger story. Recording and editing later enables the reporter to ask the same question over again if he stumbles over his words. You can do the same with your answer. The best thing to remember here is that if you start an answer and flub it after a couple of words, simply stop and start over. If they are just going to use a sound bite, the reporter is not likely to air your mistake.

- **Live in studio:** You are being interviewed in a setting in which you are with other people in the room and can interact with them as if it were just a normal conversation. This is probably the most comfortable of the three formats.

- **Live on location:** You are alone in a studio facing nothing but a camera because you are in a remote location, away from the main studio where the interviewer is located. You can hear through an earpiece but not see the interviewer. Look straight into the camera the entire time (but don't glare), just as though it were an interviewer. If you look away, you'll seem distracted and aloof. Keep looking at the camera until the technician in the studio says you are off the air.

- **Television interviews** generally are as much about style as substance. With some exceptions, there is little room for asking in-depth questions that require in-depth answers. So how do you get your story right? Make sure the reporter is well briefed on the subject. TV reporters often have to cover a wide range of topics. The better informed they are, the better questions they will ask and the better the interview will go. You don't want a reporter asking, "So, what does your business do?" Better to get a question like, "After 20 years in the business, what trends do you see for the next year or so?" Schedule a background phone call before the interview, if possible, to cover all of the basic information with the reporter.

"Style vs. substance" reminds me of something that happened to me years ago. I once took the CEO of a company on a media tour to talk with newspaper reporters and TV and radio hosts in a few cities. While in Cleveland, I booked the executive to do an interview at the city's largest TV station. Everything was set except that I had forgotten to ask who the other guests on the show would be.

As luck would have it, preceding our CEO was a then-very-young pop singer Debbie Gibson who was as bubbly as a sugared-up eight-year-old at a birthday party. Following her was Heather Whitestone, who—in addition to being deaf, poised, beautiful, brilliant and charming—happened to be the reigning Miss America. They both looked incredible on camera and were big hits.

Then came our guy who—although he did a good job in the interview—was (and for all I know, still is) your standard-issue, middle-aged man in a dark suit. Had I known who the other guests were, I'd have asked that my guy appear first so as not to follow these two celebrities. I don't remember much of what anyone said on the show, but I do remember how loooooong and quiet our taxi ride was back to the hotel.

I'm Not an Actor, but I Play One on TV

Here are some rules to remember when doing a television interview:

• **Before you do a broadcast interview, make sure you have all of the details.** Who is doing the interview? Will it be a panel interview on a particular topic or will your executive have the camera and/or mic to himself? Know the show format and the names of other guests who will be on before you. (See the consequences of not doing so in the paragraph above.)

• **Memorize your message points.** Don't look at your notes. Repeat messages two or three times naturally during the conversation so the interviewer can choose the best versions of sound bites.

• **Sit slightly forward** in an upright, non-swivel chair with arms.

• **Men: Wear dark suits with off-white or blue shirts.** Avoid "busy" ties. Sit on the bottom of your suit jacket so the shoulders do not ride up.

• **Men: Don't refuse makeup.** A little powder on the forehead will keep you from looking like a lighthouse. Bring an electric shaver to erase your five o'clock shadow. Wear socks that go up to your calf so your ankles don't show.

• **Women: Avoid large, shiny, dangling, or otherwise distracting jewelry.** Avoid "busy" clothing patterns. Colors are fine.

• **Be visual.** Do the interview at your place of business, if appropriate. Even better, if you have a factory floor, a control room, or some other kind of high visual, use that as the backdrop.

• **Bring a prop** — your product or some other object to illustrate your point.

• **Talk directly to the interviewer.** The camera and microphone will find you. Maintain eye contact.

• **Gesture with your hands where appropriate.**

• **Be personable and open. Smile when appropriate.**

Master the TV Interview: Have Something to Say and Look Great Doing It

There's an old adage that television adds 10 pounds to anyone's appearance. I think it really depends on how many jelly doughnuts you eat in the green room before the broadcast. Maybe thecamera does give you a slightly wider appearance, but how you look depends more on yourposture, your face, your gestures, and the way inwhich you dress. More important, the broadcastmedium slightly flattens an interviewee's personality. In normal conversation, for example, whensomeone is making a point, you listen and occasionally nod your head in agreement or disagreement.

On television, the temptation is to stare off into space as the lights and cameras bear in on you. Stay relaxed, pay attention to the interviewer, and be engaged, bright, and personable. Also, don't nod your head constantly (even as a sign that you understand the nature of the questions), or it will appear as though you are agreeing with everything the interviewer is saying.

Still the best example of the power of an appearance on TV is the oft-cited 1960 John Kennedy-Richard Nixon debate. Nixon had a five o' clock shadow, looked awful, and appeared distracted. Kennedy was fit, tanned, and dressed in a dark, well-fitting suit. He looked like a movie star. Polls showed that people who watched it on TV thought Kennedy won. Radio listeners gave it to Nixon. I've always suspected that, even on radio, one could tell that Nixon needed a shave.

Worksheet: TV Pre-Interview "Style" Checklist

- See Chapter 14 for tackling the substance of any media interview – getting your messages into the story.

- Arrive to the studio early to catch your breath and assess the entire set including the chair, audience, lights, mics and other environmentals.

- Greet the interviewer and the show director

- Men: if wearing a jacket, sit on the lower back of the jacket so it does not ride up at the collar.

- Women: avoid jewelry that is flashy and distracting.

- Men: don't refuse light makeup

- Never sit in a swivel chair. Ask for a stationary chair with arms.

- Relax, smile, use your hands to gesture, be conversational in style and substance but stick to your messages.

- Be yourself

16

Master the Radio Interview

"Radio is the most honest, direct and intimate medium we have. It is just one person, in a room, talking into a microphone. There is no better way for one person to speak to many." – **Marc Fisher**

Chapter Summary: Whisper Sweet Somethings in Their Ears

1. Radio is the most intimate medium. Take advantage of it by having a one-on-one conversation with the audience.
2. When pitching a radio story, give the producer a new angle on a topic that the station's listeners have not heard before.
3. You can give a radio interview by phone from your home, your office, or even—if the station will let you—your cell phone.
4. Keep your important messages in front of you as you speak.
5. Be descriptive. Paint a clear and vivid picture for the listeners.
6. Keep answers short. Don't be intimidated by silence. You are not responsible for dealing with gaps on the air; the interviewer is.

As a businessperson looking for visibility, radio is still a spectacular medium, one that you should explore as a means by which to increase your visibility. According to the National Association of Broadcasters, there are more than 15,000 radio stations in the United States. They reach more than three quarters of all Americans over the age of 12, and more than a third of adults listen to radio while at work. If you are a national company, that kind of coverage gives you ample outlets in each of your important markets through which you can gain visibility.

Marc Fisher, author of Something in the Air, says, "Radio is the most honest, direct and intimate medium we have. It is just one person, in a room, talking into a microphone. There is no better way for one person to speak to many."

Even in an age when one can hear music on practically any devices except a toaster, there is still something magical about riding in your car or sitting in your kitchen and listening to the radio. It's just the announcer on the radio speaking directly to you and you alone. Or a favorite song coming in loud and clear as though it were live.

So, as a business person trying to communicate with your audiences, radio is hard to beat. Besides the intimacy of the medium, a big plus of using radio to gain visibility is that there is no need to travel. You can give a radio interview from your home, your office, or even your cell phone. Contrast this with TV, for which you at least have to go to a local studio or, if you want to be on numerous talk shows, you have to travel from city to city to get on the air.

How to Get Yourself on the Radio and Get Noticed

- Decide whether the news you have is big enough for a national program (the likes of National Public Radio or one of the big network programs) or a local program. Most likely, you'll aim for a local talk-news station.

- A great resource for finding stations in your region is radiolocator.com, an international online directory that enables you to search quickly byZIP code, state, call letters, format, or evencountry. Click on a station's call letters,and it takes you to its website. Spend afew minutes looking at various radio station websites. Note their format (talk ormusic).

- Check the websites of all of your local stations. Determine which ones have interview programs that reach your audiences. If you are not familiar with the stations, ask friends and colleagues for advice on which would be best to pitch with your story.

- All-news stations generally are good for business stories but you should, by no means, limit yourself to that format. Try for morning or afternoon drive time since those nearly always afford the highest listenership. The station with the highest ratings may not necessarily be the best one for you. If you have a story that you think would appeal more to a Spanish-language or African-American oriented station, by all means put that station at the top of your pitch list.

How to Pitch Your Radio Story and Make It into Drive Time

Most radio stations have assignment editors, producers, or on-air hosts who determine which guest, stories, and topics will get on the air. At smaller stations, you are more likely to get through to a producer by phone. Larger stations are more accessible by email. Call the station and find out whom to pitch to. In any case, you want to be ready with the following information that the decision-maker will need in order to decide whether to pursue your story:

• **The local news hook**—what makes you and your topic worth putting on the air?

• **Show that you are familiar with the talk-show host.** Note that you have heard their programs and think your topic would be a good match.

• **Controversy is the key to the kingdom.** Give the producer a new angle on a topic that the station's listeners have not heard before. I once heard a promo for an upcoming radio news program that starting with something like "Iced tea: Can it hurt you?" Online we'd call that click bait.

• **Go through the same exercise that was mentioned above in Chapter 10** about brainstorming story ideas. For example, if you are a tax lawyer and Congress has just passed legislation that provides for three new deductions, be the first to pitch the story to your radio producers.

• **Exhibit a sense of humor if the topic is appropriate.** Show them in your pitch that you can be entertaining and lively. A good guest, like a good host, keeps things moving quickly and colorfully.

Painting a Vivid Picture for Listeners Will Help You Be a Great Radio Guest

Here are some guidelines to help you ace a radio interview once your pitch is accepted:

• **Before the interview,** let your clients and potential clients know that you will be on the radio. Send them the information via email and on your social media platforms a few days before the event. Also notify reporters who cover you and your company regularly.

• **Listen to the show(s)** on which you are going to appear. Familiarize yourself with the interviewer's style.

• **Keep your notes in front of you.** Have your five or six main messages (see Chapter 4) ready to go and use them generously. Remember, that's why you are doing the interview.

• **Keep answers short.** Don't be intimidated by silence. You are not responsible for dealing with gaps on the air; the interviewer is. The late CBS newsman Mike Wallace was asked why he often pauses after an interviewee provides an answer. His reply: "They get embarrassed by the silence and they begin to fill the silence. Suddenly, they really begin to talk." Don't do that.

• **Speak directly in a normal voice** to the interviewer and the audience; your personality will come through.

• **Smile** — you will sound more friendly.

• **Be descriptive.** Paint a clear and vivid picture for the listeners. If you are opening a new store in town, for example, instead of describing it as "hundreds of square feet," try "the size of the average Starbucks."

• **Don't be overly promotional** unless the specific topic of the interview will be your organization, your product, or your service. If you are there because of your expertise on a particular topic, you can slip in a subtle plug though. Also, the host will introduce you as president of the XYZ Co., and will mention your product or service as part of the intro to the interview anyway.

• **If it is a call-in show, expect a few crazy questions. Roll with it.** Exhibiting a sense of humor will do more to stop the crazy calls than being outraged and letting it show. Zip right back to your main messages.

Have someone record your radio interviews with quality equipment and get permission from the radio stations (in writing is best) to post them on your website. Often, stations will send you an audio file of your interview if you request one. Some charge for the file. Pay it; it is worth every penny to be able to post the interview on your website. In any case, you can link to the interviews on their websites if they have online archives.

The Radio Tour

You can get on the radio in multiple cities in a single day by doing what is called a "Radio Tour," in which you set up numerous radio interviews ahead of time and, one by one, they call you to put you on the air live. It's a great gig and an excellent way to be in more than one place at a time. There are plenty of companies that will help you set up a "radio tour," that is, they will book you on radio programs in various cities and, in the majority of cases, you can do the interviews over the phone. **(See "The Satellite Media Tour" at the end of Chapter 12).**

Worksheet: Radio Pre-Interview Checklist

- See Chapter 14 for tackling the substance of any media interview – getting your messages into the story.

- Arrive to the studio early to catch your breath and get focused.

- Remove distractions. Turn off cellphone.

- Bring a written list of your most important messages. Since you are not on camera, you can keep these in front of you for reference.

- Speak normally, the engineer will make sure that the mic is placed properly.

- Be conversational

- Smile. It will make your voice sound more friendly and personable.

Handle Media Crises Like a Pro

"There cannot be a crisis next week. My schedule is already full." – **former Secretary of State Henry Kissinger**

Chapter Summary: Hope for Sun, but Buy an Umbrella

1. Create a short and readable crisis plan, an outline that covers possible crises, actions to take, messages, and spokespeople. Review the outline at least a couple of times a year with staff.
2. Get to know reporters during the good times so you can work with them more effectively during a crisis. If they respect you personally and professionally, you will almost always get better treatment when there is a problem. At the very least, you'll have a better opportunity to tell your side of the story.
3. Warn your important audiences (senior staff, board) when the company is about to do something that might generate controversy and/or a crisis.
4. If a crisis breaks, stick to your plan. Be as open as possible with information to press and other audiences, especially to employees.

Ever notice how actors, rock stars, socialites, business magnates, and other celebrities say something in public that appears to be ignorant, shortsighted, and career-ending, and then, after a few weeks of getting bashed in the media (and lots of free publicity) it turns out to be only ignorant and shortsighted? Celebrities pay their handlers big money to help them make crazy mistakes. Meanwhile, they are invited onto every talk show to explain their gaffe (and sell their new movie, book, TV show, or CD). A year later, they do it again.

The Chinese symbol for "crisis" is the same as the symbol for "opportunity." Makes you wonder, if they have thousands of symbols, why do they need to double up? But I digress. Anyway, even centuries ago, the Chinese and other cultures recognized that a crisis, handled properly, creates an opportunity to affect change in a positive way.

Media crises can be excellent opportunities for good PR as long as no one is going bankrupt, to court, to jail, or to the emergency room. Even a few months in jail or rehab are no biggies as long as you are rich and famous. In fact, they can be real career-builders—but I am certainly not recommending them.

Misery, Your Company's Here

"Paying is for the little people." How does that statement make you feel? Me? Angry, particularly around April. But that's what the late über-hotelier Leona Helmsley allegedly said to her domestic help before she was jailed for fudging on her tax bill while the rest of America was filling out 1040s. Was anyone sad when she went to the pokey? TIME magazine ran her photo on the cover with a caption that read, "Rhymes with Witch."

Martha Stewart—who cultivated an aloof, bulletproof, perfectionist persona—was in a similar situation. She lied about illegal gains from insider stock trading, and ended up with a five-month sentence for what humorist Dave Barry called, "taking her down a peg." However, all is forgiven: Stewart is back on top, signing deal after deal, getting her lines of products into stores, and doing quite nicely, thank you.

How Tylenol Handled a Major Headache

This is one of the most-cited examples of good crisis PR and you should know about it -- the Tylenol poisoning case in the 1980s. Someone had added cyanide to containers of its product on store shelves in Chicago. Tylenol immediately got word out to the press to warn the public and pulled its pills from the market nationwide until the cause was determined. The cost was in the millions, but the lives and reputation they saved—and the good PR they received—were worth millions more.

It did not take long before Tylenol's market share rose higher than it was before the crisis. The lesson here is that people perceived that the company was as concerned with public health as it was with the company's bottom line. It shows good judgment, iron will and a high regard for the general public. And Tylenol did it even before there was social media to get the word out.

Hallmark Knows How to Say "I'm Sorry"

Here is one I especially like. Imagine that you are the world's biggest greeting card company with a website that enables people to send electronic greeting cards. Now imagine that the whole thing crashes on Valentine's Day! That's exactly what happened to Hallmark. People tried to send e-cards to their sweethearts and all they got was a message saying the system was down because of an Internet traffic jam on their site. OK, so it was not a life-and-death situation, but it was a service promised and not delivered.

Had Hallmark ignored the snafu, it would have been the last time most customers would try to access the site. Instead, within a couple of hours after discovering the problem, they sent out an email to everyone who attempted to send an e-card. It is so perfectly written that I have to quote it here. Granted, if anyone should know how to say they're sorry, it is the writers at Hallmark. Nevertheless, they get an A+ for being responsive, fast, and contrite.

Here is the email: "Dear Friend, We owe you an apology. First, the most important three words of this letter—WE ARE SORRY. This Valentine's Day, our site was up and down all day. For many of you, that meant frustration and wasted time when you were simply trying to send or retrieve an e-card. We thought we were ready to handle a huge amount of traffic on Valentine's Day. Obviously we thought wrong. We were surprised by double the amount of traffic we expected. And we cringe at the disappointment we caused some of you. In short, we made promises to deliver that were not kept. And for those of you who experienced that disappointment, we are so sorry for any frustration we may have caused. Rest assured this experience will serve as a lesson for us. We are now challenging our team to reevaluate every step we took for Valentine's Day because it wasn't enough. With our deepest apologies, The Hallmark.com Team."

Try Your Best Not to Cause an Oil Spill, But….

Why can't companies that inflict real pain do the same thing? Try this: read the same paragraph but pretend it is an apology from Exxon for spilling oil all across an Alaskan shoreline. That letter, posted online and run as a giant ad in The New York Times—no more than 48 hours after smacking the reef—would have made a profound and positive impact. The ecological damage would still be there, and so would the negligence, but at least the company could have demonstrated its concern immediately for the gravity of the situation.

Long before you have a crisis, build personal relationships and solid two-way communication with representatives of each group that affects your company. For example, if you are going to put up what appears to be a smokestack, but the emissions will be only steam, let environmental groups and nearby residents know before it happens. They still may not like the idea, but at least they will feel you are being honest with them. You might even put up signs on fences around your property that say "Stack emissions are steam."

The same goes for employees. Let's say you just had to fire 5% of your staff. Explain why. "Profits are down and, for now, we need to trim staff and travel, and stop new equipment purchases. We do not anticipate any additional layoffs." The latter is most important. In times of crisis, employees care first about themselves and then about the company. They want to know, "How will this affect me?"

Make sure you understand who your primary audiences are in a crisis. they may include one or more of these stakeholders:

• **Customers** who are disappointed with your performance

• **Regulators and legislators** who have the power to restrict your operations and markets

• **Environmental groups** that may oppose your waste processes, packaging, products, and land-use practices

• **Shareholders** who suspect improprieties or object to particular executive hiring or poor investment decisions

• **Neighboring businesses or residents** who object to any of your activities

• **Employees** who may charge unfair hiring or promotion practices, unsafe working conditions, or other similar complaints

• **Your board of directors**

• **Your investors**

• **Your business partners**

• **Your vendors**

What to Do NOW to Prepare for a Possible Media Crisis

• **Get to know reporters** during the good times so you can work with them more effectively during a crisis. If they respect you personally and professionally, you will almost always get better treatment when there is a problem. Or at least, you'll gain a better opportunity to tell your side of the story.

• **Warn your important audiences** (senior staff, board) when the company is about to do something that might generate controversy and/or a crisis.

• **If you predict that you are about to get some negative press, warn senior staff** and the board that there might be an article in the paper.

• **Get your "champions" up to date** and ready to speak with the press if necessary.

• **Planning:** Ask yourself, "Does my company have an oil tanker off the coast of Alaska?" "An aging nuclear power plant?" If you can answer "no" to these questions, good. Try a few more.

• **Age, gender, and race discrimination:** How do we stand? How many women and minorities are on our executive staff and board?

• **Environmental concerns:** What is our record? How would our practices look in a front-page story?

• **Product recalls:** Is there an accident waiting to happen?

• **Financial improprieties:** Do we have the right checks and balances? Who's watching the books with enough guts to tell the boss (or the board) that something is amiss?

• **Staff:** Do we know of people in the company who have a record of violence, dishonesty or other bad stuff? This is a sensitive issue that involves privacy, so if you are going to act on it, do so carefully. Get HR and Legal involved early.

Follow an Open and Well-Organized Crisis Strategy

Let's say your company rarely gets major press attention and now comes your worst fear: negative publicity over wrongdoing by your company. Assume, for example, that your CFO has been accused of purposely over-reporting profits to boost the company stock price. The bad news gets out, your stock price drops, and the regulators and press—smelling blood in the water—start circling. You have only one chance to get it right. Consider these two scenarios:

a. You impose an information blackout. No one talks with the press after your general counsel says the company did nothing wrong. You hunker down and hope it will blow over. It won't.

Or, a second scenario:

b. You sideline the CFO pending an investigation and install an outside accounting firm to look into the matter. The CEO holds a short news conference to answer questions about the alleged discrepancies (those he or she can legally discuss) and keeps the public and press informed as developments unfold. You issue a public statement with your main messages that 1) accountability is paramount in the company, 2) in the company's 50-year history, there has never been a similar incident, and 3) you intend to get to the bottom of the allegations. In the meantime, you presume there to be no wrongdoing.

The first scenario will lead to wild theories in the press that you will have to deny eventually, and will foment mistrust. It won't go away on its own. The second scenario actually gives you an opportunity to show that you are concerned with the problem and have the best interest of stockholders, customers, employees, and other audiences at heart. Handled properly, it may even give you an opportunity for positive press that you did not have before.

I am not suggesting that you sacrifice your CFO or anyone else on the altar of public relations, but if a problem occurs, move quickly to fix it and be forthright with the public about how you do so.

Tactics That Will Help You Weather the Crisis Storm

Take out your crisis plan. No, not the 40-page tome that you will never read, but a three-page list of steps you will take to deal with a crisis. Update it every year. The crisis plan should include:

- **Messages:** Four or five main messages for every possible crisis scenario.

- **Spokespersons:** The names of public spokespersons and members of the crisis team.

- **Facts Keeper:** The person who will brief staff on the problem as soon as possible.

- **Tactics and Strategy:** A clear articulation of your crisis strategy.

- **Plan:** An hour-by-hour, day-by-day schedule of activities.

- **Materials:** Statements, fact sheets, template letters, Q&A and news releases that address the most likely crises.

- **Contacts:** A list of home, office and cell phone numbers of all crisis team members.

- **Phone numbers:** For all possible suppliers, partners, investors and subcontractors who might be involved or will need to know about the situation.

- **Champions:** People who can speak positively on your behalf.

- **Staff huddle:** Meet with principal staff to get all of the facts. Give them each a copy of the crisis plan. Go over it together briefly.

- **Close to the vest:** Do not email the plan or your messages during a crisis. Soft copies have a way of finding themselves in the hands of reporters. If the crisis is bad enough, the crisis plan and the messages will make a great negative story of its own.

Before you act, calm down, close your door, block distractions and read your crisis plan.

• Review your main messages.

• Role-play with staff. Answer every conceivable question they can muster. Force them to be tough on you.

• Remember, you can manage the news, but you can't control it. Don't try.

• Resist the temptation to fire off a scathing letter to a reporter or paper that runs a particularly negative story. Write the letter if you have to, carry it in your pocket for the rest of the day, and then shred it. You'll feel better and you will avoid the possibility of a PR train wreck that makes you look thin-skinned.

• Inform staff via a brief email. Make it short, professional, and noble because the chances are very good that someone will give it to the press. In fact, write it with that possibility in mind.

• Tell the truth. Never lie to a reporter. However, you are not required to tell him or her any more than is necessary to get your point across. See general interview pointers in Chapter

• "No comment" does not mean no story. Get in front of the press. Tell them you will brief them when you have the facts, and then do so before deadlines approach, if possible.

• Never repeat the negative phrase in a reporter's question. It will end up as part of your quote. Reporter: "Don't you think you are cheating the stockholders?" You: "We are not cheating the stockholders." Next day's headline: "Joe Smith: XYZ Co.: 'We Are Not Cheating Stockholders.'" The better answer might have been: "We've weathered downturns before. Customer and shareholder value is one of our top concerns."

• Be as cooperative as possible with reporters. But be cautious.

• If there is another company involved—let that company's representative speak for his or her own team—but coordinate your information, your messages, and your activities.

• Never go "off the record." See Chapter 18.

• Follow up with the reporter. This is part of being cooperative. Ask him or her if the information you provided was clear.

• Do what you can now to correct the problem and make sure the press and staff know about the fix. Also announce any long-term improvements, if possible.

18

Don't Go off the Record or Into Deep Doo-Doo

"Drawing on my fine command of the English language, I said nothing." **-- writer Robert Benchley**

Chapter Summary: "No Comment" Is a Comment

1. Going on and off the record during an interview is sure to get you into trouble. Don't. There is too much room for error on the part of the reporter.
2. If you need to talk without being quoted, give the reporter an entire off-the-record briefing to give him or her the background and context needed to understand your company, industry, product, or service.
3. If you are misquoted, decide whether it is worth it to demand a correction. How important was the mistake? Call or email the reporter to point out the error and move on.

Off the Record is a Dangerous Place

There are only a handful of people who understand the nuances of doing interviews "on background," "deep background," or "not for attribution." This kind of intrigue happens frequently when government officials are being interviewed regarding a controversy. They want to get their views out there to help sway public opinion, but they don't want to be—or are not allowed to be—quoted. Generally, here is what the terms mean:

• **"Off the record"**: I will tell you in order to provide some perspective, but you can't use the information for publication.

• **"Not for attribution"**: You can quote me but only as a "senior administration official" or other such title that can't be traced back to me.

• **"Background"**: You can paraphrase the information only in general terms, not indicating that you got it from anyone in particular.

• **"Deep Background"**: What conversation?

• **"Deep Throat"**: Let's meet in the big, dark garage while the creepy music plays. I liked it better when I thought actor Hal Holbrook was the real Deep Throat. Fun fact: the garage where Bob Woodward and Mark Felt (the real Deep Throat) met is located in Arlington, VA and has an historical sign marking the location.

Here's the good news: You don't need to remember any of these distinctions unless you become such an influential newsmaker that your mere quote can send the stock market plunging and Air Force jets streaking into the sky. All you need to remember is that, as a businessperson learning the media ropes, you should never go "off the record" during an interview. You rarely gain anything by doing so.

Most of the people who talk on background, deep background, or other such nonsense are mid- or junior-level employees who get an ego boost by talking to big shot reporters. It's called "leaking." There is a time and place for leaking information, but it's tricky and if you are not experienced with the media, it can backfire.

Leaking is often done as a "trial balloon," a way to test an idea or a position on an issue. Instead of the President announcing an idea, for example, an underling will leak it to a reporter under "not for attribution" rules. The story ends up reading something like, "A source in the Treasury Department has told The Daily Beast that the federal government is thinking of changing the color of money to blue." If the idea is a big hit, then it is safe for the President to announce it formally. If there is an outrage over the idea of blue money, the idea may be scrapped.

All Kinds of Trouble

Here's why you should stay "on the record." Let's say that in the middle of an interview, a reporter asks you a question that you don't want to answer. She asks you to tell her anyway "off the record"—that is, just for her own information. She says she will not use the answer in her story. But here is what can happen:

• The reporter gets confused with her notes later because she forgot to write that the answer was off the record. You get quoted. Uh-oh. Angry phone calls are then exchanged between you, the reporter, and her editor.

• The reporter gets the same information "on the record" a few days later from someone else and decides to use that information because now it is public. Uh-oh. Angry phone calls are then exchanged between you, the reporter, and her editor.

• The reporter does an end-run around you to one of your colleagues or bosses. For example, you give the reporter the information "off the record." She then goes to one of your colleagues and asks for "on the record" answer to the question. She gets it. Uh-oh. Angry phone calls are then exchanged between you, the reporter, her editor, and your colleague.

If you need to educate a reporter on your company or your industry, but you don't want to be quoted, it is best to make the entire conversation a "backgrounder"—much less confusing for all parties. All of the notes from that conversation are not for publication and the reporter is less likely to misunderstand the distinction. Still, I have always found it a good practice never to say anything to a reporter that you would not want to see on the front page of the paper.

They Quoted Me Saying What?

After your story comes out, you still need to play by certain rules to maintain good press relations. Let's assume that your story turned out great and made you and your company look like stars. It is fine to call a reporter and thank him or her for "diligence and fairness." But never thank a reporter for writing a positive story; it's not their job to make you look good. Thanking them for giving you kudos makes them feel like second-class journalists.

Never send a gift of any kind—most newspapers won't let reporters accept them anyway. A short note or email is fine. Once the story appears, thank the reporter for taking an interest in your company, for taking the time to learn about your product and service, and for presenting the story fairly. The best thank-you gift you can give a reporter is a great story tip and the names of experts with plenty of information. Be a source of good story ideas.

What to Do With a Negative Story

What if you end up with a negative story that you feel you did not deserve? What is your recourse? Despite the fact that there are a number of ways to seek redress, none of them are particularly good. Unless you and the reporter or editoragree that the reporter's work was so inaccuratethat it was a total misrepresentation, forget abouta lengthy printed correction. And even if you doget one, who reads them? The original story may have appeared on page one, but the correction will be buried elsewhere.

Choose your battles! If the story says you have only 100 employees instead of 130, or if the story says that you work only with government agencies when the truth is that you have a couple of corporate clients, forget it. Suck it up and move on. It never hurts to call the reporter and tell him or her about the mistake. At least it won't happen a second time.

If there was truly a major error or you disagree strongly with the conclusion of an article or column, by all means talk with the reporter about it and ask for a correction. Also, you can write a letter to the editor or even a bylined column on the topic that, at least, does get readership. Better yet, have someone else—one of your champions (See Chapter 13)—write one. Having a third-party endorsement is more convincing than your own.

One of my most memorable episodes with a reporter consistently "misquoting" sources came when I worked for a brand-new news magazine. On our staff was an unflinchingly opinionated reporter from Europe (where advocacy journalism has been an art form for centuries) who covered European affairs. Given the time difference, he was pretty busy in the morning trying to reach officials in Europe and Scandinavia.

His M.O. was to ask questions that went something like this: "Wouldn't you say that the [name of a political party] are nothing but a bunch of pathetic whiners?" We'd crowd around his desk listening in on the speakerphone while the person on the other end answered something like "Uh-huh," or "Oui." A few days later, his story would include a quote, "Minister of Finance Jean LeJones recently called the [name of a political party] "nothing but a bunch of pathetic whiners.'"

19

The Only Reason to Hold a Press Conference

"A recent survey stated that the average person's greatest fear is having to give a speech in public. Somehow this ranked even higher than death, which was third on the list. So, you're telling me that at a funeral, most people would rather be the guy in the coffin than have to stand up and give a eulogy?" – **comedian Jerry Seinfeld**

Chapter Summary: Managing Expectations—Do You Really Need a Press Conference?

1. Don't sentence yourself to a press conference unless you have convinced yourself, beyond a reasonable doubt, that a press conference is the best way to communicate your news.
2. You may wish to call the event a "briefing" to lower expectations.
3. Consider a virtual press conference—a teleconference or webcast—as an alternative.
4. You need news, a VIP if possible, and an interesting/unusual

venue to help assure success.

5. Send out an advance advisory to editors with all of the details. Follow up with phone calls.

A press conference can be a useful tool for getting press attention. Reporters can't afford to waste time. If they come to your press conference and if you meet their information needs, they will almost always write a story. At a news conference, you reach many reporters at once with a person-to-person message. And the fact that you have filled the room speaks to the importance of what you have announced. That's what it should do.

But Wait, There's More to This

Unfortunately, that is not always the case. Some press conferences are dismal failures akin to doing a standup comedy routine only to realize 10 minutes into your act, with your brow dripping in sweat under the lights, that the audience speaks only Swedish and you don't.

Suffice it to say that if you have ever held a press conference where no one showed up, it is not something you want to repeat—just you, your boss, and a few colleagues devouring the little carrots and cheese wedges on the snack table in a big, empty room.

There are many reasons not to hold a press conference— so many, in fact, that we could devote an entire chapter to the topic. But we'll pick only a few:

• Your boss/staff/spouse/chairman would like you to do one.

• Your competitor just did one and it was successful.

• Your staff wants you to do one.

• It has been months since the last one, which was successful and productive.

• You just joined an exclusive business club and they have an impressive meeting facility.

Factors that can destroy turnout at a press conference:

• Bad weather

• Good weather

• No real news

• Conflicting last-minute events that take priority over your news

• Wrong day of the week and/or wrong time. Go early in the week and early in the day. (No Fridays!)

• Too many "I will try to make it" RSVPs from reporters

• Inconvenient location

Again, reporters are notoriously busy people. Asking them to drive or cab over to the other side of town and sit through your presentation is A Big Ask. It had better be good.

There is Only One Good Reason to Hold a Live Press Conference: You have news to announce that will be of high interest to reporters who reach your intended audience. You have a reasonable expectation that the news—plus the timing, location, and conditions—will be such that you can expect a good turnout and subsequent positive coverage of what is said, and you will get more attention by holding the event than you would have otherwise.

Some Guidelines for Conducting Press Conferences

- **Scheduling conflicts:** Before you schedule a press conference, look at every local online event calendar you can find. Do your best to make sure you are not competing with anything that is going to draw the very press you are trying to attract. Call two or three reporters who cover your company or industry most closely and call colleagues in other organizations to ask them if they know of anything that might conflict with your planned event.

- **The End of the World:** Even after doing that, Murphy's Law dictates a 50-50 chance of having a giant meteor crash into the Earth 30 minutes before your press conference is about to start. Reporters will be distracted from your press conference by the prospect of a new Ice Age and the end of life on our planet. Unless, of course, they cover sports or show business.

- **Food:** You may wish to call the event a "briefing" to lower expectations. If you do, make it more informal: fewer invited press, fewer staff in attendance. If it is a morning event, provide coffee, drinks, and light food— and advertise in your press advisory that food will be provided.

  Oh sure, reporters and everyone else will pretend that food does not matter. But most reporters are human and, like all mammals, they come to the muddy riverbank at sunrise to drink coffee and eat muffins. If the event is in the afternoon, provide snacks and soft drinks. Never serve alcohol.

- **Celebrity:** Besides big news, the best draw at a press conference is A Famous Person. We all know this, of course, because we are drowning in information about celebrities. However, it is always fun and interesting to see the phenomenon up close.

- **More Celebrity:** This one really stuck in my mind: At a press conference some years ago to promote a TV program about space exploration, for example, organizers had onstage an active-duty female NASA astronaut (truly, a rocket scientist) and—for some reason completely lost to me now— then Star Trek actress Kate Mulgrew, who played (pause for Google search) "Kathryn Janeway, captain of the Federation Starship USS Voyager" and, later, a prison inmate in the Netflix series "Orange is the New Black."

After the presentation, the press horde and other attendees (including a couple of members of Congress) pushed forward to meet—you guessed it—Mulgrew. Meanwhile, the real astronaut was completely ignored until a few stragglers wandered over (probably to ask whether she had ever met Leonard Nimoy).

- **Newsworthiness:** In addition to whatever good they do for their favorite cause, famous people draw reporters to events because everything they do is deemed to be newsworthy. Outside of New York and Hollywood, visiting actors are big news. Outside of Washington, visiting U.S. Senators are big news. Outside of Key West, Jimmy Buffett is big news.

  You get the idea. Second best are people who, although not famous, are seen as unique in a particular media market. For example, the head of a national Native American organization or a group of coal miners at a press conference in Hollywood would attract attention. Or just invite George Clooney.

- **Diversity:** Choose a diverse mix of speakers—by gender, race, discipline, politics—so reporters and other attendees will have a variety of people to interview at the end of the event. Also, it makes for a more compelling presentation. Make presentations brief—generally, a press conference, including the question period, should last no more than an hour.

- **Make it Easy to Access:** Livestream it or make a video and audio recording of the event. Post it online and link it to your website and social media platforms.

- **Shiny Trucks Make a Good Background:** Pick venues that will make stories more colorful, especially for television. If your story is about a medical breakthrough, have the news conference at a conveniently located hospital or research lab. If it's about a new software product that helps fire departments respond quicker, hold the event at a fire station with the big, shiny trucks in the background.

- **Think in Color:** Reporters are more likely to attend events at unusual venues than at another drab hotel conference room. Choose baseball stadiums, ice rinks, department stores, airplane hangars, sawmills, candy factories, and similar places. Think color! Provide a good visual backdrop for cameras—something that will illustrate your news—perhaps a banner bearing the name of your organization or product.

- **The Satellite Media Tour** Before or during the time reporters are arriving at your press conference, give them copies of the following: fact sheets, news releases, names and titles of speakers, marketing materials, white papers, press clips and press contact names. (Provide only the PR person's contact information; you do not wantreporters calling company executivesdirectly. That way, you can prepare the executive to do the interview.) The easiest way to make this material available, of course, is to post it as pdf. documents on your website and provide a link before the event.

- **Take Names:** Be sure to have a sign-in sheet, and collect business cards as a backup, to ensurethat you can follow up with every reporterwho attends your press conference to seeif they are writing a story and to offer your assistance should they need additional information.

- **Taking Questions:** How many questions should you answer at a press conference? A very general rule of thumb is to answer as many as you and your team feel will satisfy reporters involved in the particular issue you are addressing. But it is always good to leave them wanting a bit more. Do your best job, cover the most important ground and then thank everyone for coming...and going.

The Virtual Press Conference: Can You Hear Me Now?

A good alternative to the in-person press conference is a webinar or even a conference call, the latter being accessible by cellphone even with less-than-perfect cell reception.

Sending an Advisory to Editors and Following Up by Phone Will Give You the Best Results

An "Advisory to Editors" is a simple press release about an event that includes only the basic facts and little narrative—mostly the five Ws of basic journalism: who, what, when, where, and why. Whichever format your choose for your press conference, send an advisory to editors and reporters in advance of the event—a week ahead is plenty of notice. Then send out another one the day before the event.

Send it by email to:

• **Reporters** at local newspapers, magazines and broadcast outlets.

• **Calendar editors** at local publications. (Most regional and local papers have a calendar column of business-event listings.)

• **Associated Press "Daybook":** AP provides a list of upcoming business, political, entertainment, and other events of interest to reporters who cover those beats. Getting your event accepted into the daybooks will increase your chances of getting reporters to attend. Go to the AP press release site: ap.org/pages/contact/contact_pr.html, find your region's AP office, and submit your advisory.

You should follow up your advisory with a call to reporters who are most important to you. This helps to keep their attention on the event and it emphasizes the fact that you think their attendance is important. If it is a big event and you have a long press invitation list, hire plenty of help to staff the phones.

Get Out of the Office!
Networking is Great PR

"One handshake is worth 250 votes." – **former President Lyndon B. Johnson**

Chapter Summary: Nothing replaces face-to-face introductions

1. Networking is work but it can be fun. Treat it that way.
2. Join one or two organizations, attend their events, and join a committee. It's better to be active in a couple of organizations than to be an occasional drop-in at many organizations. Be "family."
3. Regular networking gets you seen as a player.
4. Come armed with a great elevator speech that says, "Here is what I can do for you."
5. Don't just collect business cards. Have more meaningful conversations with fewer people rather than trying to work the whole room.
6. Follow up with good contacts a day or so after an event. In a week, they will have forgotten you.

If Woody Allen is right—that "70% percent of success in life is showing up"— its application to business success is the act of networking. In fact, because of the power that electronic communications gives us to than before. Nothing replaces in-person meetings—not videoconferences, webcasts, texts, phone calls, emails, or any other type of electronic social networking.

We get hundreds—thousands—of online "introductions" from faceless strangers selling us product and services galore and most of it is spam. *But when you network, the act of shaking someone's hand firmly, looking them straight in the eye, and telling them what you can do for them is still the most direct and powerful introduction in business.*

A Good Networking Encounter Might Be a First Meeting with Your Future Customer

Make networking an integral part of your public relations plan. HR professionals will tell you that hiring managers decide whether they like a job candidate within the first two minutes of the interview. Networking provides the same "advantage," if you will.

You're at an industry meeting, you meet a potential client, and, within a minute or two, they will at least know whether 1) "you are a pleasant person I might want to work with," 2) "you have the skills to help me accomplish my goals," and 3) "you are probably active in my industry because you are at this event."

So, in essence, you've already had your first meeting. You make an appointment with the person and, when you see each other next, you already have some positive impression about each other and you have something in common to talk about: the event you both attended.

Networking puts you in the right place at the right time. At a big convention once, I literally bumped into a senior executive I had met a few months earlier in his office to discuss a possible PR campaign.

He was coming around one corner of an exhibit and I was coming around the other corner, and we nearly knocked each other down. After laughing about it, he gave me his card and said he was now with a new company and would I come by his office to talk about PR for his new organization. We met a few days later and I got the work.

After nearly eight years, that executive—the one I almost knocked over in the aisle—is responsible for references to his and other companies that have made up nearly 20% of my billing. It was a lucky collision, sure, but you have to put yourself in lots of different networking situations for luck to "happen."

Networking helps you make new contacts, keep tabs on industry developments, pick up new ideas, and meet prospective customers, partners, investors, employees, and employers.

Tips to leverage networking into your public relations efforts:

• **Before an event, find out who is going to be there.** If an organization is important to you, ask the host to introduce you. Big events are not always better. Go for quality over quantity. Collecting a bucket of business cards is of no use. You'll have spent five seconds each with dozens of people instead of a more productive amount of time with a smaller number group. But, don't spend all of your time with just one or two attendees either. Break off conversations politely and work the room. Stay out of the comfort zone of talking only with people you already know.

• **Be a familiar face:** Going to events, over time, makes others see you as a "player," someone who is involved in the industry, the local business community, and, of course, the organizations that sponsor the networking events you attend.

• **Frequency:** A couple of outings a month is probably optimal. In theory, you could go to a worthwhile business breakfast, lunch, and dinner event every day. You'd be well connected but your cholesterol would be in the low four figures. It is much better to pick one or two organizations and go to their events frequently than to spread yourself over many groups and just show up to each one a couple of times a year.

• **Exposure:** Be a sponsor if you can afford it. Keep your organization's name in front of all of the members as much as possible.

• **A Team Effort:** Everyone on your team should attend networking events as their time permits. Find out which organizations members of your team already belong to and encourage them to be active. Determine which other organizations your team should join.

• **The Benefits of YOU:** Get your elevator speech down: Be able to tell networkers in 15 seconds what your company can do to help them succeed. It may sound to you as though a fellow attendee is asking, "What do you do?" but what he or she is really asking is, "What can you do for me?"

• **Join a committee:** Being part of the "family" rather than just attending events gives you access to information in advance. On the membership committee, for example, you'll be the first to welcome new members (and possible prospects).

• **Split Up:** If you go to an event with other members of your team, split up during both the networking period and the event itself. Sounds obvious, but often coworkers will all sit together at the same table. That's a waste of time.

• **Line of Sight:** Wear your nametag on the right. When someone shakes your right hand, they will be automatically looking at your badge.

Follow up with people you meet within one or two days, while their memory of the event is still fresh. Remind your contacts who you are, what you do, what you discussed, and, again, how you can help their organizations.

Guy Kawasaki, one of the most visible business writers around said in Entrepreneur magazine, "In my career, I have given away thousands of business cards. The funny thing: hardly anyone ever follows up. Great schmoozers follow up within 24 hours—a short email will do." He adds, "Include at least one thing that shows the recipient he isn't getting a canned email."

Where to Network

Every region, large and small, features business and civic groups that provide excellent events for networking. Depending on where you live you might also have chapters of organizations that represent your industry such as trade associations and business councils. Here are a few organizations to consider, as a start:

- **Meetup Groups:** there is a meetup group for virtually every interest imaginable from business to sports to the arts to travel and thousands more. Register online at meetup.com, choose a group or two to follow and soon you'll be receiving notices of gatherings.

- **Chambers of Commerce** bring business people together and, as a whole, help to grow the regional business community. Most have excellent events. Great place to meet business contacts. It's always best to choose one or two chambers, join a committee or two, and help out rather than just attending events and heading out the door.

- **BNI** (an international networking organization) is a surprisingly large and active network with chapters in dozens of countries and throughout every state. Each chapter features only one person per profession so there are no competitors within individual chapters. BNI's more formalized organizational structure can be beneficial – members are expected to attend their chapter meetings every week or send a substitute. Some chapters meet for breakfast and others lunch. Guests are strongly encouraged to attend. Some chapter members earn a significant percentage of their annual income from the connections they make in their chapter and region. Each week members have the opportunity to talk about their businesses to the entire group and, after a relatively short time, they get to know the strengths of each member of the chapter and guests that attend. Get more information at bni.com.

- **Rotary and other service organizations:** These are great places to make contacts but keep in mind that their primary purpose is public service – not passing business referrals -- but that latter happens naturally of course and chapters can be a great source of contacts.

- **Alumni organizations:** These provide a natural affinity – you automatically have something in common with event attendees and will be considered "family." Most bigger colleges and universities have alumni groups in just about every major urban area. Others have chapters wherever there is a strong concentration of alumni. These are especially great for young people looking for mentors as well as potential internships, jobs and social gatherings.

Worksheet: Networking Events Checklist

- **How many networking events can I realistically attend in a month?**

- **What time of day is most convenient for me?**

- **What is my target audience?**

- **Which organizations with networking events have the highest percentage of that target audience? Register to receive event email notices from each of these organizations.**
  - o **1.**
  - o **2.**
  - o **3.**
  - o **4.**
  - o **5.**

- **Month** _____
  - o **Event:**
  - o **Event:**
  - o **Event:**

- **Month** _____
  - o **Event:**
  - o **Event:**
  - o **Event:**

14 Things You Must Do to Win Visibility and Succeed at Trade Shows

"We didn't lose the game; we just ran out of time." -
- **football coach Vince Lombardi**

Chapter Summary: Bring a Solid Strategy with You to Trade Shows

1. Pick the events, large or small, that will enable you to reach prospects who matter most.
2. Book a good booth location or skip the convention.
3. Get the attendees list ahead of time and choose specific people/companies you would like to contact. Ask conference organizers to make introductions.
4. Get the press list ahead of time and send reporters an email telling them why they should be interested in visiting your booth.

5. Make your booth inviting and professional.
6. Assign a staffer to keep all contacts' business cards and other contact information. Follow up quickly.

If you think the concept of "The Invisible Man" is science fiction, try getting attention in a booth with 1,000 other exhibitors at a trade show attended by 40,000 people. I have worked the press function at scores of trade shows both as communication director of the company that is sponsoring the show and as a press representative of companies exhibiting at a show. Sometimes, months after an event, I wake up in a cold sweat, dreaming that my company is exhibiting at yet another giant Las Vegas convention. Our booth has nothing in it and no one staffing it.

Avoid this nightmare. If you are in charge of deciding which trade shows your company will attend, you need to consider a number of factors. Not all of these are of the PR or marketing nature, but before we talk about maximizing PR attention at a trade show, we should spend a few minutes talking about which events to participate in and how to get high visibility out of them.

Before the Event

Pick the Right Events and Skip the Rest

Make a list of all of the major and secondary trade shows in your industry. Winnow the list down to those that will be attended by potential customers and, if possible, press. Choose only those that give you the most for your money. Trade show organizers can give you some idea of the types of people who will be attending. The most important factor in choosing a show how well your products or services solve the problems of those who are attending.

Be Realistic About Your Budget

There are a lot of expenses associated with a trade show: the booth, the exhibit itself, travel, lodging, printing materials, staff time (and lost staff time back at the office), temp help if needed, shipping, and setup costs. For each show, make a detailed list of all expenses: shipping the booth, air travel, logo shirts, booth fees, meals, hotel, transportation, press outreach, etc. Make an educated guess, based on the people who are attending the convention: How many prospects can we expect for x dollars spent?

Decide in Advance What You Want to Accomplish

Come in with a specific strategy and stick to it. Decide in advance what you want to accomplish. Are you selling products on the floor or taking orders? Are you making appointments with potential customers? Are you collecting qualified leads for later? Generally, you need at least two people to staff a trade show—one to be in the booth at any given time and another to cruise the show during quieter times, checking out potential customers at booths, on the display floor, and among speakers and attendees at the sessions.

Also, don't pass up the opportunity to look at your competitors up close. You can learn a lot about them in this kind of situation. This is not spying. It is market research. OK, it's spying.

If You Can Smell Soft Pretzels, You're in the Right Place

Get a good location on the exhibit floor or skip the show. "If we were just attendees at the show, would we visit our booth?" Unless your booth is near an entrance, in an aisle, or within smelling distance of the food court, you will be relegated to one of the bleakest rings of trade show hell—"the corners where no humans walk"—the fourth dimension of the big convention, if you'll excuse the mixed metaphor. You will be wasting your money, wasting your time, and killing your sales force's morale.

Don't be tempted to go, even if they give you the booth space for free. Book early and demand prime real estate. For worthwhile shows, if you can afford it, buy a bigger booth. A 10'x10' space is fine, but a larger one will make a better impression if it is properly outfitted and staffed.

Get the Attendee List and Pick Your Targets in Advance

Determine what constitutes a qualified prospect and how many you can expect to attend. Get the attendees list in advance. Make a list of all of the companies you want to connect with and assign each person a share of the targets. This is critical. The true value of trade shows is that many of your potential clients, partners, investors, vendors, etc., will be in one place at one time.

If you have been trying to get a meeting with someone at XYZCo. and they are likely to be at the conference, make it a point to assign someone to find the XYZCo. rep and have them work to set up a meeting during or after the show.

If you can't get this year's attendees list before the show, check last year's list which will most likely be posted on the convention website. Call the organizers in advance (far in advance, not two days before the show when they are frantic) and remind them that you are a paying exhibitor and that you want to meet John Doe of XYZCo. during the event. Will they make an introduction? The right answer for a competent show organizer is "yes."

Prepare Follow-Up Letters Ahead of Time

Create a "nice-to-meet-you-at-the-show" template letter ahead of time and have it ready to mail-merge with your list of contacts as soon as you return to the office. Important attendees should receive a follow-up letter within a few days of the event.

All of the Reporters You Want to Meet Will Be in One Place

If meeting press is one of your goals, make good press attendance a criterion for attending the event. Remember, if you are exhibiting, you are a paying customer and you're entitled to certain perks (or "perqs" if you want to be more accurate). One of those is getting the registered press list in advance.

Get the press list about a week in advance if possible (even though it won't be complete since some scribes show up without registering).

Choose the top 10 reporters (the ones who work for publications your prospects read, not necessarily just The New York Times). Send every reporter a customized, one-paragraph email (seriously, one paragraph) telling them why your product or service will be of interest to their audience. Look at the show schedule, note periods of downtime, and suggest appointments during those periods. Exchange cell phone numbers so you can reach each other at the event. Give interviews and demos at the booth, if possible. If that's not possible, find a quiet place to talk. Promise them interviews that will take only 15 minutes and stick to the bargain. Don't take up their time unless you really have something to show them.

Daily Convention Newspaper: Direct Line to Reaching Attendees

Most big conferences have a daily newsletter that is distributed to all attendees. It is referred to as the "show daily." A few still provide a paper version, but mostly it is done via email or an app. If you are going to announce some news at the show, give it to the editors a week ahead of time so they can be sure to include it on the day you make the announcement. Remember, many attendees are your prospects. Reach out to them in every way possible including Twitter.

During the Event Make Your Booth Inviting by Opening It Up

The biggest failures at trade shows occur when staffers fall into the comfort zone of hanging around the booth, sitting in chairs set aside for prospects, eating lunch and talking only to each other. This is off-putting and intimidating to visitors.

When you need a break, go somewhere else. Trade shows done properly are hard work. They require attention to prospects and a willingness to make the same short speech over and over for days. Open your booth space as much as possible; make it easy for people to walk in without the feeling of being trapped. Once they are in, you can then ask them if they would like information.

Note Contact Information Carefully

This is so important—the real reason you are here. Make collecting and sorting contact information a formal process, not just a byproduct of sitting at the booth. At any given time there should be someone in the booth who is assigned to collect business cards and, on each one, note the nature of the conversation, interest in the product or service (use a rating system of 1 to 5), and any other important information. Ask everyone for a card.

Be tenacious. One of you should be assigned to take these cards home—in a pocket or a purse—and ensure they do not get misplaced.

Promote Your Company and Booth with Wild Abandon

Watching fireflies at night is instructive in putting together a trade show strategy. How do fireflies distinguish one another? How do they find each other and mate successfully on a hot summer night? Entomologists say different species have different patterns of light blinking. Frankly, they all look the same to me—the entomologists, I mean. So do trade show exhibitors.

What can you do to draw attention to your company? If you have a comfortable budget, it is easier, of course. Sponsor lunches or dinners, advertise on the sides of convention shuttles, create big banners, and take out an ad in the event book.

If your budget is smaller, you will have to use more imagination, but it's more fun. Let's start with a few easy ones: models, munchies, and merchandise.

1. Models: Hire a couple of local models, dress them in your company-logo shirts and have them give away flyers that describe what your product can do for anyone in the industry that the trade show represents. Have them invite people to the booth.

2. Logos: Everyone on your team should wear a company-logo shirt. Do you have local interns, young relatives, kind friends, or other people who may have some time to give you? Dress a small army of people in your logo shirts and send them out onto the floor to hand out brochures. Have small thank-you gifts ready to give them at the end of their tour of duty.

3. Hi, My Names Is: Everyone on your team should wear a name tag.

4. Energy Booster: Instead of candy at the booth, put out cookies or brownies. Few people can resist them, especially after 3:00 in the afternoon when everyone's energy is low. Give your models a plate of cookies and product brochures and send them out onto the floor.

5. Prizes: Have a drawing for something of real value every day: the iPad mini and Fitbit as prizes have been overdone. Try something new. A GPS? A high-quality bluetooth speaker? If you are going to put your company name on something, use objects that people will actually keep along with the usual pens and sticky notes.

6. Luggage Tags?: One of the best booth draws I have seen are little laminating machines that make luggage tags out of business cards. People love the tags and will line up at the booth to get them, especially for their laptop bags. I never would have believed it had I not seen it for myself. Yes, I did wait in line for a luggage tag.

7. Giveaway: Don't offer up a free month of your service as a prize. A free trial period of 15 or 30 days should go to anyone who is interested. That's the point of getting them to the booth. Give away trial registrations at the same rate you give away cookies.

8. Take photos. Whenever someone important gets near your booth (said the spider to the fly) draw them in and snap their picture surrounded by staff in logo shirts with your booth in the background. These will play well on your website with a descriptive caption. If you really want to get as much use out of the photos as possible, have people sign an informal "model release" so you can use the shots in marketing materials. A written note from them giving you permission to use the photo in marketing materials is usually sufficient but check with your legal counsel.

9. Compare notes: Modify your strategy as needed. All of your conference staff should meet briefly at the end of every day to compare information and impressions. Adjust your show strategy accordingly.

After the Event Contact Your Contacts as Soon as Possible

Chances are, if the event is in a place like San Francisco, Hawaii, or Orlando, at least some of the staff will take extra time off and stay on location. Make sure that whoever is heading back to the office right after the show has all of the contact information of booth visitors. Upon arrival, have the information inserted into a spreadsheet and generate follow-up letters. Those who expressed interest in a meeting should get special handling such as a handwritten note or the template letter and a phone call. Time for the sales staff to do the hard work. As soon as everyone is back in the office, meet to discuss follow-up strategy. Make specific assignments and deadlines.

Press the Press as Soon as Possible

Send a follow-up email to all registered press, even if they did not attend the show. Call the ones you made contact with and ask if they need additional information and whether they plan to write anything. Keep track of pending articles so you will see them when they are published.

Publish All of the Goodies to Dress Up Your web Site

Put everything: releases, photos, articles from the show daily, insights, etc., onto your website. Make sure to include your site's URL in your follow-up emails to prospects and press.

Worksheet: Countdown to Launch
One hour before the trade show or conference starts:

- Look at our booth. Is it open, friendly and inviting?

- Make sure materials are out.

- End private conversations between our team members. Focus on the attendees and be ready to talk with them.

- Is our whole team "on message." Practice describing the benefits of our services or products (not just their features).

- Check with organizers to find out when important press will be at the event.

- Find out which VIPs will be at the event and make a point to invite them to the booth to learn about the company and to take a photo or two to post on social media.

Should You Hire a PR Firm? What to Know

"My greatest strength as a consultant is to be ignorant and ask a few questions." -- **Peter F. Drucker**

Chapter Summary: PR Firms and Consultants: Do You Need Them?

How and Why to Hire a PR Firm and How to Know if You Need One
1. Determine what you want to accomplish. More press? Handle a crisis? Promote a specific product or service? Better internal communication?
2. What are your needs and budget? Would a sole practitioner do the job? A small PR firm? Or a large national or international firm?
3. Get a referral from someone you trust.
4. Interview three possible firms for starters. Have a phone conversation with each and tell them what you need and what your expectations are. Ask them to come in and make a pitch.

5. Listen carefully but trust your gut. Are these people you'd like to work with?
6. Never be a firm's smallest client. Ask about the pecking order.

Public relations firms and individuals can be indispensable in helping you reach your communication goals. Not only can they provide the expertise and media relationships you may not have on your team, but they can provide valuable bench strength—more arms and legs to actually execute the work on a day-to-day basis. If they are good, they will be results-driven and accountable.

They can also be expensive, difficult to work with, and a major headache if you pick the wrong one. How do you know if you need a PR firm? How should you pick a firm? How much should you spend? How should you manage the relationship and what expectations should you have for results?

Let's dig into it.

Worldwide Lucite Shortage! You Have Four Choices for Staffing a PR Campaign

First let's look at the options available to you for staffing a PR campaign:

• Do it yourself or designate someone on your team to handle some modest PR duties in addition to their other responsibilities. This often falls to the person who handles marketing. This can be a good way for a small company to get started.

• Hire an in-house PR person with as much experience as you can afford. The cost for the right person is likely to be at least whatever you are paying a director-level staffer. Always choose people with good communication skills and experience, not people who only have expertise in your industry. Just like a good reporter can do research on and write about almost anything, a good PR person can promote just about anything. If he or she has also worked in your industry, so much the better.

• Use an independent PR consultant who can do the work at a reasonable rate — with as much experience as you can afford. Expect to pay anywhere from $100 an hour to $300 an hour depending on experience, location, and the difficulty of the assignment. A big advantage of outside consultants is that they can put together just the right team of peers to do the work without a lot of overhead. You can, in effect, hire a whole team of senior PR people.

• Hire a public relations firm. If you decide to hire a PR firm, here are the steps that will help you find a good match to your goals, your people, and your expectations:

Hiring a PR Firm: Trust Your Gut

1. Goals: Decide what you are trying to accomplish. More press? Handle a crisis? Promote a specific product or service? Better internal communication? Better press materials? Write down your objectives. Talk with your sales, business development and marketing people. Get their input and make sure your PR goals support your overall business goals.

2. Budget: Determine a budget range. Small firms will charge about $4,000 or $5,000 per month. If you want a senior team to execute a complex, national campaign for a large corporation, you will pay much more. What do you want to accomplish and how much can you afford? If you need hundreds of press calls made per week, you'll need a PR firm of some size.

3. Referral: Get a referral from someone you trust. PR is a relationship business and it is critical that you find an effective team that you enjoy working with. If you don't know anyone using a PR firm, contact the local chapter of the Public Relations Society of America or the International Association of Business Communicators. They can provide names. Many cities have organizations made up of independent sole practitioners. You can find them on the web.

If you have a couple of solid referrals, stick to them and don't worry about other firms unless the referrals don't pan out. Interview three possible firms for starters. Have a phone conversation with each and tell them what you need and what your expectations are. Ask them to come in and make a pitch.

Do not ask them to come in with a fully formed communication plan. You don't work for free, and neither do they. You should not expect them to put in more than a few hours preparing for the meeting unless you are hiring a major national firm and the expectations—and budget—are much higher. If you expect a proposal that reflects 20-30 hours worth of work, offer to pay for the time spent. In any case, never interview more than three firms at a time.

5. Principals Only: When you invite firms in for a pitch meeting, insist that only the people who will be working on the account for at least a few hours each week attend. The most frustrating practice of any professional services firm is the bait and switch: bringing a Lexus full of gray-haired senior vice presidents to the meeting and then, when you hire the firm, they throw you a couple of junior people who have no strategic experience.

6. Size Matters: Never be a firm's smallest client. If your budget is small, be honest about it up front. Ask specifically how you will rank according to your budget. This will determine how much attention you'll get. Better to hire a smaller, hungrier firm (with a good track record) that will treat you like royalty than a big firm who may forget about you every time their big clients have a crisis.

7. One Hour Meeting: The pitch meeting should last about an hour. Spend the first 20 minutes telling them about your objectives, your company, your competitors, and your team. Invite to the meeting everyone in your company who will work day-to-day on communication. Designate a single point of contact to the PR firm and let that person do most of the talking. Spend the next 20 minutes listening to the PR firm's pitch and the remainder of the time discussing strategies, some tactics, and getting to know them.

8. Trust Your Gut. Are these people you'd like to work with? Are they personable, smart, and open to suggestion or do they have a PR template that they impose on all of their clients? Did they listen carefully or did they talk too much, dropping celebrity namesand trying to impress you with their knowledge? Did they ask you how you run yourbusiness or did they tell you how youshould? How did they treat your receptionist while waiting for you in the lobby(be sure to ask the receptionist about this when the meeting is over)?

9. Ask for more referrals and check them carefully. You will learn more by asking about the results they have made for other similar clients than anything else.

10. Have your next meeting at their office. Observe the physical space and the people. Talk with some of them and get a sense of who is behind the scenes. It will reveal a lot. Meet with the president of the company and see how he or she relates to the people who will be working on your account. Again, trust your gut.

11. Don't be overly impressed by all of the awards in the lobby. Trade associations for the PR and advertising industries love to give awards. Agency lobbies are always jammed with of shelves full of Lucite obelisks attesting to every bit of work—major and minor— they have ever done. Fortunately, when they build office space for PR firms, architects design the floors with reinforced steel trusses to carry the extra load of tons and tons of Lucite awards. If ever we experience a worldwide Lucite shortage, public relations firms and advertising agencies will cease to exist and life as we know it will be impossible.

12. Initially, sign a 90-day contract. Set specific goals and deadlines. Give the firm 30 days to get ramped up and educated. They should conduct necessary research, create your main messages, and develop a communication plan that lists some specific activities. In the next 60 days, they should start getting results – maybe a few press story placements. Don't expect miracles in the first couple of months but expect some success and plenty of great ideas with which to move ahead.

13. Ask for accountability but don't overdo it. A short, informal monthly list of what the firm did during the past 30 days is important for your information and their accountability. Don't bog them down creating big reports that burn up lots of expensive hours. Remember, PR people are as good at promoting themselves as they are in promoting you, their client. If you ask them for a monthly report with multimedia special effects, you'll get one. And you'll pay for it.

How to Know Whether Your Public Relations is Working?

"In theory, there is no difference between theory and practice. But in practice, there is." **– baseball great Yogi Berra**

Chapter Summary: Half My PR is Working -- Which Half ?

1. A stack of press clips, in itself, is not a particularly accurate scale for measuring PR success unless the clips 1) appear in the publications prospects read and 2) include your main messages.
2. Surveys and focus groups can give you a fairly good indication of how well your PR activities are working.
3. A good quick way to do a poll with little expense is to survey customers and ask them what they like and dislike about your company.
4. Another good way to track ROI on PR activities is to chart the way in which sales spike in response to announcements you make.

How do you know you are getting a good return on your investment of time and money in your public relations activities? Getting a cause-effect breakdown (knowing which part of your PR is responsible for which part of the newfound success of your business) is not an exact science, but it is an art form that has developed considerably over the past decade as businesses demand to know their return on investment in every facet of their organizations.

Measuring PR is more qualitative than quantitative, but you can get a good sense of your success. Here are some methods of tracking your results to help you understand whether you are getting the ROI you deserve for your efforts.

Are Press Clippings a Good Measure of How Well Your PR is Working?

Tracking press clippings: A stack of press clips, in itself, is not a particularly accurate scale for measuring PR success unless 1) they appear in the publications your prospects and other important audiences read and 2) they include your main messages—the reason you give interviews. You can compare your clips from one year to the next, and you will get a general sense of the improvement of your PR campaign.

But don't assume that the two-pound stack of clips you got this year is better than the one pound you got last year. All clips are not created equal. A tiny mention in your big city paper will be more difficult to land than an article in a small weekly newspaper. But, for your audience—which may be your immediate neighborhood if you are a local dentist office or clothing boutique—the small weekly paper may be the better bet.

If you are sending press releases and doing media interviews, there are a number of services that will provide you with clips of articles or snippets of TV and radio spots in which you are mentioned.

First, try Google Alerts as mentioned in Chapter 6. It is free. Google provides a platform in which you can list key words (such as company, product and peoples' names. You will get an email notification when those keywords appear in a media article.

When you get an alert, note the name and contact information of the reporter who wrote it. Print-clipping services that charge a membership fee include burrelles.com and cision.com and are much more comprehensive. For clips of stories aired on TV or radio, try metromonitor.com. There are many others.

Deceptive Math

Media impressions: This is also a widely used method that, frankly, can be misleading. It works this way: You take all of your press clips and multiply each one by the total circulation of the publication in which it appeared. So, if you got a mention in The Wall Street Journal, *in theory,* you achieved 2.2 million impressions (the number of people who potentially saw the mention of your company). But this method serves only as a blunt instrument to measure your effectiveness.

First, the chances that all two million subscribers saw the mention of your company are small. Second, even if they did see it, did it register enough for them to remember you? Maybe you have achieved tens of millions of media impressions over a period of time but the numbers don't really tell the story.

Also, equating media coverage to comparable advertising is difficult to quantify. A positive story about a company holds much more value than an ad of the same size, but how much more? It depends on the contents of the story, the placement, the messages conveyed, and the publication in which it appeared.

In order to be of value, a media placement must:

• Reach the right audiences

• Make an emotional connection between your products and the audience

• Include at least some of your messages

• Leave the audience with a positive impression of your company, product, or service

• Be prominent (A small mention on the last page of the back section of the paper may not be of much value.)

Tracking messages: This method owes more to a gut feeling than actual quantification, but it can give you a better sense of the way in which your messages are being picked up. Look at articles in which you have been quoted or mentioned. Take out your message document and compare your five to six main messages with what is contained in the articles. Check off how many times each message (it need not be verbatim) appears in print. If your count is low, you know that you need to be more "on message" when you do your interviews.

Mirror, Mirror on the Wall, Surveys Tell if You Are Fairest of All

Before-and-after surveys are among of the best ways to measure awareness and attitudes toward your organization and its products, services, or issues. Look at your business and PR goals and use them to determine what you want to measure. Put together a survey that asks questions that will give you the best sense of how visible you are to your audiences and what they think of your products and services. Doing your survey on a regular basis will give you a baseline against which to measure your progress.

Depending on how big a sample you need to poll and how complex the survey, the costs will vary widely. Use what you can afford. One of the biggest polling companies, for example, is Harris Interactive (harrisinteractive.com). They include a lot of good information on their website about how organizations have used polling. Depending on your needs, you might want to start with a local company that provides research services.

Free Surveys Are a Great Place to Start

You can also create, distribute and analyze surveys online for a minimal cost, of course. Some companies even offer a small survey free as an incentive to try their services. Here are some of the sites we mentioned in Chapter 10 on using survey results as a story idea to pitch to reporters. Try surveymonkey.com, constantcontact.com, freeonlinesurveys.com or zoomerang.com.

If you have only a very few questions you need to have answered, and your budget is limited, you might be able to add some questions to other organizations' polls and ride their coattails. If you belong to a chamber of commerce or other business organization, for example, they might be willing to include your questions if they are pertinent to their membership.

Focus groups: These are used quite often in business and, as with surveys, the cost will vary with the size of the group and how complex the process is. If you have no experience conducting focus groups, you will benefit from getting an outside firm to help out. You'll need to get the right people and the right facilitator into the room, and then understand how to interpret the results.

Free Focus Grouping is a Good Tactic, Thanks to Some Online Services

Here is a method that is equal parts survey and focus group and can be done in minimal time with little financial outlay except your time. Contact your current customers and ask them five or six questions that will elicit the information you need to help measure the effectiveness of your PR. The most important aspect of this method is the quality of the questions you ask. Test the questions first on staff and other contacts.

Questions to current customers might include:

1. How has your impression of our company changed during the time we have been working with you?

2. What do you like most and least about working with us?

3. How does your impression of our organization compare with your impression of our competitors?

4. What could you read or hear about us that would raise your opinion of our organization?

5. How would you like to receive information about us (e-newsletter, direct mail)?

6. How did you find out about us?

Conducting this informal focus group or survey annually will give you a general sense of how your PR (and your services in general) are affecting your customers. Often, it is best to get someone outside your company to make the calls so customers feel more comfortable being frank. Also, have the caller assure customers that the answers will be reported anonymously.

The Echo: If your main messages are strong and your PR methods of getting them out to your primary audiences are effective, you are going to notice something interesting: Your messages are going to come back to you! You will see them in articles for which you, your customers, and your other champions are interviewed. You will see and hear them in presentations by others in your industry who have heard or seen your messages. As a result, you'll see them more and more often in web searches related to your organization.

Other Indicators That Your PR May Be Working:

• You get more press calls than before. (Also, does your call volume increase just after you send out a press release?)

• The questions you get from reporters indicate that they know more about your organization. (You don't have to explain each time what your organization does.)

• Your story pitches to reporters work more often than when you started using them.

• The information in your press releases gets mentioned in the media more often.

• Members of your team are quoted more frequently than before.

Conclusion

"The secret of getting ahead is getting started. The secret of getting started is breaking your complex, overwhelming tasks into small, manageable tasks, and then starting on the first one." **-- Mark Twain**

I hope you have using this book as much as I have enjoyed writing it. The act of researching and writing the book has helped me recall some of the most interesting and funny episodes in my professional life—all of them learning experiences. A career spent in journalism and public relations opens the door to opportunities that one might have missed otherwise. Mine has been no different. It continues to be a great ride, thanks to the terrific people I meet and with whom I am privileged to work every day.

PR Should Be Fun

Public relations is not only rewarding for any organization, it can be a lot of fun, whether it is only a small part of your job or your primary responsibility. It is certainly one of the most colorful aspects of business.

It is always great to see client organizations, their products, or their services featured prominently and positively in major news stories. Visibility brings in business and creates a strong brand. The effect on the companies' reputations, their relationships and their bottom lines over time make the effort of winning good PR worthwhile.

The secret to getting your public relations campaign started is really no secret at all. Just pick a few of the activities in this book that feel most comfortable to you and try them. You'll soon know what works best. I am confident that if you have already put into practice at least some the techniques and tactics in this book, you are no longer wondering, "How come no one knows about us?"

How it Ends and How it Starts!

Spoiler alert! If you're one of those people who read the last pages of a book first to see how it ends, here it is: Your team set its PR objectives, created its key messages, thought up and pitched great story ideas, got lots of attention from the media and other audiences, became very famous and successful, and lived happily ever after. Thousands of others have done it. So can you.

From the Author:

If you find this book useful, please take a minute to write a review on Amazon.com. To comment on the book, please send an email to robert@rdccommunication.com.

Thank you!

# # #

CPSIA information can be obtained
at www.ICGtesting.com
Printed in the USA
FSHW012036250820
73299FS